TH

SYNTHESIS
EFFECT

THE
SYNTHESIS
EFFECT

YOUR DIRECT PATH
TO PERSONAL POWER AND
TRANSFORMATION

JOHN McGRAIL, PhD

New Page Books
A division of The Career Press, Inc.
Pompton Plains, N.J.

THE SYNTHESIS EFFECT
EDITED AND TYPESET BY KARA KUMPEL
Cover design by Howard Grossman/12E Design
Printed in the U.S.A.

To order this title, please call toll-free 1-800-CAREER-1 (NJ and Canada: 201-848-0310) to order using VISA or MasterCard, or for further information on books from Career Press.

The Career Press, Inc.
220 West Parkway, Unit 12
Pompton Plains, NJ 07444
www.careerpress.com

Library of Congress Cataloging-in-Publication Data
McGrail, John, 1952-
      The synthesis effect : your direct path to personal power and transformation / by John McGrail.
            p. cm.
      Includes index.
      ISBN 978-1-60163-205-0 -- ISBN 978-1-60163-612-6 (ebook) 1. Change (Psychology) 2. Self-realization. I. Title.

      BF637.C4M336 2012
      158.1--dc23

                                                            2011045925

I joyfully dedicate this book to my wife, Lynne-Anne. Fifteen years ago, under "our tree," we took our wedding vows and pledged to live our life together with love, friendship, humor, and spirit; it has been all of that and more. I value and appreciate your constant support, encouragement, and inspiration throughout the project more than I can ever express. You are one of my luminaries; truly the light of my life, and I love you forever.

Acknowledgments

Most stories logically flow from beginning to end, but to best tell the story of my appreciation and thanks for making *The Synthesis Effect* possible, I think I need to go from the end to the beginning, as it helps me keep things in order. Before I begin, I apologize in advance to anyone who should be included here but isn't; I assure you it is not intentional, but there are just so many people I owe thanks to, I am sure I will forget some by pure accident.

First, I gratefully thank the entire team at Career Press for their tremendous support and guidance throughout the process of getting my baby to press. Of course we couldn't have met had it not been for my incredible agent, Maryann Karinch, principle owner of the Rudy Agency. Your enthusiasm for my writing, my vision, and my message has been eclipsed only by your knowledge of the business and expert guidance throughout the process of finding the right home for the book. Thank you, forever!

My profuse thanks and appreciation go out to my illustrator and friend, Dariela Cruz. Your artistry and talent gave life and spirit to my scrawny little diagrams; they look better than I imagined they could.

To my cousin, good friend, and "big sister," Professor Pat Henriquez— we've come a long way from eating 70-cent pizzas and drinking 10-cent Cokes at Zuppardi's on Friday nights with the proceeds from your paper route so many years ago—my undying thanks for oh-so-casually mentioning that I ought to meet your friend Maryann. What a great idea!

To all my clients, everyone I have had the privilege and honor to work with all these years, I offer undying and eternal thanks. Every session with every one of you helps me grow and evolve, both as a healer and as a human being; you inspire me to be the very best person I can be. Had it not been for your trust in me, and especially for those of you who said, "Dr. John, you need to write a book about this stuff," there likely would be no book.

Had it not been for the excellent initial training I received at the Hypnosis Motivation Institute in Los Angeles—one of the finest colleges of hypnotherapy anywhere—I wouldn't be doing what I'm doing; I'm forever grateful that I found you. And to my dear mentor and friend, Wendy Glenn, wherever you are, my eternal thanks and blessings for helping me rediscover my power and my path so many years ago. You also inspired me to accept the calling to help others heal their lives; there are no words that can express my appreciation for that gift.

To members of my family—Uncle Bud, Jud, Judy, Dean, Justin, Vico, and my mother-in-law, Ruth—my thanks for your love, support, and interest in what I do. Our after-dinner chats during the two-year process of researching, organizing, and writing the book were invaluable in helping me figure out how it ought to flow and what I ought to say—not an insignificant challenge.

Then there is a special member of the family, our matriarch, Aunt Irene (Aunt I, as we called her). She was living in physical, emotional, and spiritual balance, in essence doing the process of Synthesis, many years ago, long before it was popular to even mention such things. I sometimes think that perhaps it was my exposure to her indomitable spirit and hyper-positive outlook on life during all those idyllic summers I spent in New Hampshire that subconsciously planted the seed that would lead to finding my spirituality, my career, and learning to live my passion.

Finally, and most importantly, to my mom, Irene McGrail, you literally and figuratively represent the beginning of the story. I couldn't have had a better parent and role model than you. It was through your example and parenting (in very challenging times) that I developed many of my most important core values and personal attributes. You taught me much of what I know about honesty, integrity, and honor; understanding and compassion for others; and the value of working hard for something that you want. Perhaps most important, you let me find my own way and walk my own path, even when I'm sure it looked to you as though I was headed for disaster. I couldn't and wouldn't be who I am today without you, mom, and although there are no adequate words, I thank you and appreciate you from the bottom of my heart and with all my love.

Medical Disclaimer

The information, methods, and techniques presented in this book are meant to be used for vocational and avocational self-improvement. They are in no way intended to replace appropriate medical and/or psychological treatment. Always consult a qualified and licensed medical and/or mental health professional before undergoing any treatment for a medical or serious psychological condition or disorder.

synthesis:

Greek, from *syntithenai* to put together, from *syn-* + *tithenai* to put, place.

1a: the composition or combination of parts or elements so as to form a whole.

1c: the combining of often diverse conceptions into a coherent whole.

—*Merriam Webster's Online Dictionary*

...in philosophy, the combination of parts, or elements, in order to form a more complete view or system. The coherent whole that results is considered to show the truth more completely than would a mere collection of parts.

—*Encyclopedia Britannica*

Contents

Preface:
Paradise Lost?

To put the world right in order, we must first put the nation in order; to put the nation in order, we must first put the family in order; to put the family in order, we must first cultivate our personal life; we must first set our hearts right.
—Confucius

Pigeon Feather awoke to the songs of the early ones. Mockingbirds, finches, and a raucous family of scrub jays perched in the giant pine beside the tribe's ceremonial teepees of rite and passage, and had begun to sing and welcome the new day even before the faintest glimmer of light in the eastern sky lent the slightest hint to its coming.

He folded his bedroll and quickly moved to the center of the huge tent, then sat and faced the open entrance, all the while silently observed by an elder of the tribal hunters who had sat nearby in vigil throughout the night. The entry faced east, and as Pigeon Feather listened to the birds outside and watched the birth of a new day, he began to recite his long-practiced prayer of passage, awaiting the appearance of Father Sun in the eastern sky, his prearranged signal to emerge and walk the path into manhood. Across a short clearing, in an identical teepee, Little Quill, Pigeon Feather's cousin and childhood playmate, did the same, she observed by an elder of the tribal weavers.

This was a day both young people had long awaited and prepared for. On this day of the new moon after the spring solstice, just a month after his 14th birthday and on the eve of her 12th menses, or "moon," they would together "leave childhood" and be declared full-fledged, adult members of the tribe. Little Pigeon would be henceforth called Tawanna-hok, Talon of the Eagle, a name chosen by the elders for his tenacity and skill as a hunter and fisherman. Little Quill, a gifted sewer and weaver, would become Qui-eh-ha-sho-ne, Quill of the Golden Touch.

Pigeon Feather could not quell the feeling of excitement and pride that surged through him. Along with his new role as a brave, or warrior, a responsibility shared by all able-bodied men of the tribe, would come his primary vocation: hunting and fishing. He could think of no greater gift he could have been chosen by the Creator to give back to his people than to be a provider of sustenance. In the neighboring teepee, Little Quill felt much the same. Along with her role as a caretaker and mother (once and if she married), her hands would create beautiful clothes and ceremonial regalia for the tribal elders and shamans, as well as birthing and funeral blankets. Hers too would be a position of great honor.

Yet neither one of these young people would garner any more esteem or special treatment than any other member of the tribe. All adults, including the chief, contributed in their way to the welfare of the tribe based upon their particular talents or abilities. It had always been so.

Almost from birth children of the tribe were allowed and encouraged to discover their natural gifts and aptitudes as they grew. They did this through watching the adults at work, and participating in games and activities based upon the necessities for survival and perpetuating tribal culture and lore. Each individual was allowed to find his or her particular talents, and then would be raised and guided to develop those gifts. Thus, he or she could not only feel important and respected, but also provide the greatest input to the welfare of the community at large.

This custom, along with a central and unshakable philosophy of living in unity and balance with nature—the earth, the sky, the waters, all the creatures of creation, and the spirit of creation itself—had held the people in good stead since the days of the ancients, "before time began and the Great Spirit and Creator breathed life into us, his children," as they said.

After what seemed like an eternity to the young people, the first rays of Father Sun finally peeked over the distant hills. Pigeon Feather and Little Quill finished their prayers, rose, and bowed toward the attending elders in silent honor, then exited their respective teepees of rite and passage (one for men, one for women).

They met on the trail between the two tents, greeted one another with a subtle nod of respect, then together turned and preceded west, the direction of growth, creation, and the passage of time as witnessed through Father Sun and Mother Moon's transits across the heavens, the Great Oneness. Together, followed by their sponsors, they walked down the trail back toward the village to be welcomed into the tribe as adults.

The celebration and ceremony of passage from child to adult took place at least once a year, usually in the spring. It was always a great day of ceremony, games, song, and dance, all capped with a grand sunset feast at which the initiates into adulthood, sometimes one or two, and sometimes more, would be introduced to the tribe by their new adult names.

As Qui-eh-ha-sho-ne, Quill of the Golden Touch, and Tawanna-hok, Talon of the Eagle, were formally introduced to the tribe, they stood tall and proud, knowing that they would serve their people for many, many years in the best way possible. The verdant valley echoed with songs of praise for the gifts of the Creator, the wisdom of the Ancients, and these new community members. The celebration and dancing continued long after Father Sun had settled into his bed beyond the western horizon.

米 米 米

This tribe and scenario I have described is fictitious, but based upon truths. It is emblematic of what are often simply called the "old ways" by contemporary descendants of indigenous peoples and cultures around the world. Theirs of course, was a simpler time. It was also a time of very different values and thinking. For the ancients and native peoples around the globe, a strong community would ensure their survival and their future.

Yet, whereas community and cooperation were essential for survival, there was another important aspect to the philosophies and lore of these peoples that far transcended just surviving from day to day. The notion of living in close connection to, as part of, and in balance with the natural world, acknowledging and embracing the concept of a spirit or essence of life that moves through and connects all things and creatures, was as central to these peoples' thinking and conduct of life as was their sense of community.

It doesn't take a rocket scientist to realize that most of us in modern society no longer live by the old ways, and we haven't for a very long time. The apparent consequences seem both starkly evident and, to many, more than a little frightening. Just looking at any newspaper or listening to most any news broadcast today will quickly affirm this perception. The contemporary Western models of science, politics, philosophy, and religion have been in practice for the last 450 years or so, but can be traced all the way back to the Ancient Greeks. Western thought emphatically rejects the old ways of living in unity, in harmony, and with spiritual connection to the natural world.

Ours is a science and philosophy that has been firmly grounded in the notions of empiricism, isolation, and distinction among systems, entities, and elements, throughout the universe and even within an organism (for example, mind and body operating as separate and distinct "parts" or "systems" within an individual). It espouses separateness from and dominance over nature, as well as separateness and dominance over one another, as individuals and as societies and cultures. We, humanity-at-large, are suffering for it both individually and collectively.

In his wonderful seminar, "Your Three Bodies," Bryan Hubbard, a London-based journalist and philosopher, cites recent studies that point to isolation as the single most significant cause of emotional stress and distress in modern society. For most of us, isolation of one sort or another begins quite early in life. Unlike the old ways of the tribal cultures, our children are very often not cherished and prized for their particular talents and aptitudes. They are also often not raised to make best use of those talents as a way to thrive and as way to ensure the greater good of their community. In fact, most kids today are not even allowed to have a real childhood, to be just average kids.

They are instead raised and encouraged to compete, excel, and dominate: Be the best, be number one. They are quite often (and often at an obscenely young age) forced into educational, athletic, or career paths chosen for them by their parents. Do all these little ones really want to be the next Tiger Woods or Michael Jordan, David Beckham, or Kristi Yamaguchi? Do they really want to be so-and-so MD or so-and-so Esquire? Quite often, they do not—not at all—but they succumb to the expectations of those who want it for them, and maybe see a future payday for themselves as a reward. Whose life is it anyway?

A few years back, I worked with a young man named Tim, a law school graduate. Tim came to me in desperation for help in passing the California Bar Exam, which he had failed in three previous attempts. I work with test anxiety a lot, and usually we get great results; we can eliminate excess stress and build a powerful flow of confidence, focus, concentration, retention, and recall. The exam becomes more like a game and less like a threat; scores go up, often by a lot.

During Tim's intake interview, when I asked him about his choice of career, he quickly confessed that what he *really* wanted was to attend culinary school and become a chef—the mere mention of which put his parents into an apoplectic fit. For generations, every male in his family had been an attorney, and it was law school and the law or nothing! His spirit was crushed and it was thus no surprise to me that he had failed the bar exam so many times. Because he consciously did not want to practice law, subconsciously he sabotaged his passing the bar exam. No therapy can make you want what you do not want.

We often self-sabotage when forced down a path of life that is incongruous to our inner being or genuine self, what we might call our core values. I see it repeatedly, in careers, athletics, and even in relationships. The impetus behind this phenomenon is what has become the bedrock of our society and mass consciousness: rampant egoism, a ravenous hunger to achieve validation through competition, material possessions, and the perception of supremacy.

Material wealth and perceived social status and celebrity—however gained—seem to be the prevailing standards by which much of our society judges a person's worth and how individuals judge themselves. We are told we need to be better than, wealthier than, more popular than, prettier and sexier than, and so on. If or when we do not wish to, or perhaps are not able to live up to those expectations for whatever reason, we self-sabotage our lives and assume the mantle of "a failure."

Many of us succumb to the pressure and learn to judge our own self-worth by what others expect or think of us, by what we do for work, or by how much money we make, where we live, or what we drive. The collateral damage is often a complete lack of personal happiness and satisfaction with one's life; a life defined by chronic stress, anger, depression, anxiety, low or no self-esteem, addictive behaviors, and dysfunctional relationships. Moreover, it all seems to be accepted by many if not most people as unavoidable; the cost of doing business as a human being in contemporary society.

In today's society, there is also a general belief that life is supposed to be a struggle, full of challenges, trials, and tribulations. For most people living in the 21st century, life is a circumstance jam-packed with pain, suffering, and obstacles we must contend with, try to survive, and overcome, rather than a miraculous process to celebrate and relish, and within which to flourish and thrive in abundance. We are a society raised on the dogma of "no pain, no gain." Where on earth did *that* come from?

We are inundated by a seemingly endless and pervasive torrent of negativity through the media: "Stay tuned for another disaster...details at 11:00." We look for instant gratification on every front, the latest silver bullet to fix whatever ails us. This sort of thinking is integral to our mass consciousness. And it obviously isn't working too well.

We are at war with ourselves in many places around the globe. We are also at war with terrorism; we are at war with famine; we are at war with innumerable diseases old and new, and some of the ones we supposedly conquered are reemerging. We are at war with other inhuman and inhumane conditions: drug abuse, poverty, injustice, intolerance, prejudice, genocide...and on it goes. Sadly, we do not seem to be winning any of these wars. Thus, as a society and as individuals we are terrified, depressed, stressed, anxious, obese, insomniac, and angry: very, very angry.

In many areas, certainly in my home of Los Angeles, there is a seemingly constant undercurrent of anger smoldering and ready to explode at the slightest provocation. Linger even an extra second at a traffic light after it turns green and you can expect a line of wigged-out drivers behind you to lean on their horns and mentally vaporize you. Since when did a few seconds make so much difference? Just what were they going to do with the five seconds of time that they actually lost? What is the rush? To where is everyone rushing? Where is the finish line?

A local professional sports team wins a championship and thousands of "fans" riot in the streets, setting fires, looting businesses, and destroying property. It does not so much look like a celebration as an excuse to vent their rage.

We are also reaping the proceeds of decades of unbridled greed, suffering under an international financial crisis of almost unprecedented proportions. At the same time, we are witness to a growing environmental crisis in global warming and climate change that many think may be irreversible.

If humanity continues on this path, it seems likely that our individual and collective psyches, our individual and collective health and wellness, and the health and wellness of the Earth itself must and will further atrophy. We suffer from endemic physical, emotional, and spiritual disconnection, living in and overcrowding a planet many believe is on the verge of environmental collapse.

Many writers on the subject of the human condition report and reflect the chilling position of numerous scientists and environmental experts who are actually predicting that the sixth mass extinction in the history of the planet may be imminent. This one will not be the result of some natural disaster: Humanity will unleash it, and the victims will be us. Some believe it is inevitable.

Is it, really? Is our paradise lost? Are you—are we—doomed to a life of pain, brokenness, and disconnection, or worse? Here are my answers: No, our paradise is not lost; *we* are. And no again, you and we are not necessarily doomed; you and we can find our way back. You and we can create a life of health and vitality, love and happiness, peace and security. You and we can eliminate our disconnection and return to our natural and desired state of wellbeing, balance, and abundance. I have devised an efficient and powerful protocol that I call the McGrail Method of Quantum Synthesis, or more simply QS Therapy, or even *more* simply, and from here on, Synthesis—a simple, pragmatic, and powerful process that can help you change your life more quickly than you might imagine. It can actually be fun, and why not? One of the central tenets of my entire philosophical outlook—Rule number 1 in the McGrail Method—is that life is supposed to be fun. What does that mean? You will find the answer in the Introduction, as we begin our journey together.

I take great joy in presenting this, and I sincerely hope it results in great joy for you once you absorb and begin to use the tools in your own personal way. Enjoy the journey!

John McGrail, PhD
Los Angeles, California

Introduction:
Life Is Supposed to Be Fun!

There is only one success—to be able to spend your life in your own way.
—Christopher Morley

"I'm unhappy." "I'm anxious." "I have no confidence." "I can't concentrate." "I can't stop smoking." "I can't sleep." "I'm in pain." "I'm afraid to fly." "I can't lose weight." "I want a relationship." "I have stage fright." "I procrastinate." "I'm afraid of men." "I'm afraid of women." "I can't take tests." "I can't have sex." "I'm heartbroken." "I hate spiders." "I can't drive anymore." "I feel unworthy." "I'm broke." "I'm stressed." "I'm depressed." "I'm lonely." "I'm afraid." "I hate my life." "I hate the way I feel." "I'm a failure."

Chances are, as you are reading this, one or more of those statements (or something like them) might be resonating with you, and maybe you would like to change that. If so, I'd like to help you. As a clinical hypnotherapist and personal empowerment specialist, I work with hundreds of people every year. My clients represent the entire spectrum of professional and socioeconomic backgrounds. People seek my help in making a change to some aspect of their lives. The list of issues in the previous paragraph is a small but representative sample of the kinds of problems my clients wish to overcome.

As you can see, the desired change may be behavioral, emotional, physical, or spiritual, and most often involves some combination of these areas—what I call the pillars of the human condition. My clients find me because they are in pain; something (sometimes many things) in their life feels broken and they cannot seem to un-break it themselves.

Most people who get that way (and that would include almost everyone in one way or another and at one time or another) feel worse in their situation because they mistakenly believe themselves to be unique, both in their pain and in their inability to fix themselves. So one of the first things I do with every new client, often before their first visit, is to reassure them that they are not at all alone in feeling stuck and in pain in their issue. I also assure them that most people need a little help becoming unstuck. It is simply a result of evolution and the functionality of the human brain and the attitude of mass consciousness in Western society that somehow sees weakness in needing help to solve a personal internal, emotional, or habitual problem. I suppose we can thank the Puritan Ethic for that notion.

One of the next points I make is that, contrary to what they may think or feel right at the moment, life is not supposed to be painful. Quite the contrary; life is supposed to be fun. I always state this with total aplomb and lots of enthusiasm; let there be no doubt here: *Life is supposed to be fun!*

I do not pretend to know exactly what that means for any given individual; we all have our own definition and version of what a fun life is. Whatever it is, it is most likely *not* an unending succession of hedonistic indulgences and it most definitely is *not* supposed to be painful, drudging, lonely, or a constant struggle.

We are all equally deserving of a happy, peaceful, loving, joyful, abundant existence. I tell them—and I absolutely believe this—that it should be a pleasure to get out of bed in the morning, to look forward to whatever the day holds in store, and then go about living it with enthusiasm and happiness. Will it be perfect? Of course not, but it can and should be mostly wonderful.

Quite often, the initial response I receive is a somewhat blank, almost quizzical stare, sometimes with a little concurrent sideways tilt of the head; a tacit but clear, "Say what?" I believe this expression is a universal response to something baffling, confusing, or incongruent, and one that is not unique to people. We often see our dogs display a similar reaction when confronted by something particularly interesting, unfamiliar, or confusing to them.

Of course, we cannot know exactly if that is what our dogs are experiencing when *they* do that, but it is indeed most often the case with a new client because I can and do ask why this notion seems so foreign, and they can and do answer me. For most, the idea of life being a truly enjoyable, abundant, fulfilling, happy experience—fun, in short—is simply absurd because it is exactly the opposite of what they have learned to believe.

Moreover, life as fun is not at all what they have experienced, and they have the emotional and behavioral dysfunctions and scars to prove it. "Buddy, after I tell you what I've been through, let me see you say that again with a straight face. Life is supposed to be fun? Are you kidding? *Humph, mutter, mutter,* and more *mutter.* Phooey; maybe I want my money back!"

I always stick to my guns on this point, and from that seminal moment forward, the whole process of our work together, the whole therapeutic enchilada, so to speak, is focused and centered on one key goal. That goal is to have them unlearn what they have grown to believe and experience, and relearn that life is not only supposed to be fun, but also that anyone and everyone— let me say this again—*anyone and everyone* has all the resources within them to make it just that.

My work, my passion, is to help my clients find and utilize those resources, and, most often, they do so in a big way. Resolving their initial issue, regardless of what it is, opens the floodgates to further growth and empowerment. I take immense satisfaction in watching a client leave my office after his or her last session with a glowing smile, expressing and projecting a completely new energy of purpose and control in his or her life. This usually occurs within a short period—sometimes only a few sessions throughout a few weeks are enough. And therein lies the purpose for and of this book.

In these pages, I will share what I've learned through my own journey and what I teach every client I work with about how to make life not just fun, but also joyful, peaceful, prosperous, and full of love and abundance of any and every sort one might desire. When you learn how and then choose to take control of your life, everything about it becomes more...well, more fun! Redundant, I know, but quite true.

The models, tools, and techniques that I have developed and bring to bear in this process were given the term *Synthesis* for a reason. In any context, *synthesis* is the bringing together and combining of parts, sometimes rather diverse parts, to form a coherent whole. That whole, if constructed well, shows the "truth" more completely than the constituent parts taken separately. (You have no doubt noted that the word *truth* appears in quotes. There is a reason for that affectation that will become clear later. For now, I ask that you simply keep it in mind as you read. Don't worry; I'll remind you about it anyway when the time comes.)

GENESIS

The genesis of Synthesis was my lifelong curiosity about the human condition, primarily in terms of the interrelationships among science, philosophy, and theology. I gravitated to science at an early age and always had a particular predilection for biology and psychology. As a teenager, I would spend hours thinking about the apparent incongruity between the easy-to-grasp empirical evidence of the science I was learning in school and the often quite esoteric religious doctrines I had been taught as a boy.

I found the theory of evolution, supported as it was by seemingly overwhelming if not indisputable scientific evidence, far more believable than the creation theory espoused in the Old Testament and taught in catechism. The notion of God as some score-keeping über-parent who sometimes doles out very tough love never really felt sensible to me. God, as a pure and infinite consciousness, the essence of all creation and life itself, seemed much more realistic and practical, even if it was difficult to visualize.

By the time I was entrenched in my undergraduate studies at Cornell University, majoring in biological science with a minor in psychology and communication arts, I had become quite philosophical about it all. For instance, when I was first exposed to neurobiology, I was (and still am) enthralled with the notion and apparent irony of the human brain trying to figure itself out! I also came to believe (and I do not know how or where this notion came from) that someday science would indeed discover the essence or secret of life itself, and in that moment we would really become one with God, thus reconciling the gap between religion and science as well as the idea of us having been created in His image. As you will see, I believe that this reconciliation is actually happening!

That curiosity eventually blossomed into a passion that resulted in a 20-year process of intensive questioning, exploring, learning, and personal growth, all initially ignited by my own issues and dysfunctions. As a younger man, I was very much one of those individuals for whom life was anything but fun or enjoyable. Throughout early adulthood and well into my 30s, I was an incredibly intense, Type-A personality, an addicted smoker, and tremendously insecure on many fronts—overall not a happy camper.

We all know the old saw, "opposites attract," and there is some truth to that. It is also true that insecurities attract. In that vein, I managed to enmesh myself in an ill-fated and ultimately very painful marriage. We were two nice people who simply did not belong together and who fed off one another's insecurities, and we did it for far too long. I had a lot going on and *a lot* to learn, and somehow, blessedly, I found the courage and the spark to do so. After one particularly momentous, break-the-camel's-back marital train wreck, I came to my senses, filed for divorce, and decided to rediscover who I really am, and what I'm really supposed to be about.

This process has included investigations and research into a variety of subjects: the sciences, primarily biology, anthropology, psychology, sociology, and physics; ancient and contemporary philosophy; theology; spirituality; metaphysics; even a bit of mysticism. Synthesis is thus an amalgam; it is of and draws from all these disciplines and more.

It was actually through and because of my personal journey, what I like to call my rediscovery of me, that I eventually found the inspiration and inner vision to pursue a career as a therapist, healer, and spiritual teacher. I initially chose hypnotherapy because it is such a powerful way to create behavioral, emotional, habitual, and physical change at a profound level, and usually quite quickly.

I will explain how hypnosis works, but please do not think that this is a book about hypnosis. Hypnosis is a powerful tool, but only a tool. What this book is about is learning how to use the power of your mind and your personal energy to change whatever it is you wish to change about your life. Whether your issue is big or small is irrelevant.

In presenting Synthesis, I will share some of the highlights of my discoveries within the various disciplines I mentioned, as well as some of my personal experiences when and where I think it might add to your growth and understanding. As I mentioned and freely admit, I found my way into this vocation not only through the course of pursuing my natural interests and curiosities, but also through a self-serving desire to have a better quality of life. I really did not like feeling broken. If you're feeling broken, I'm guessing you don't like it either.

It was as I achieved that better life and learned how to maintain it and continue growing that I came to the inspiration to help others do the same. Throughout the years I have been in clinical practice I have been called many things by my clients and pupils: teacher, therapist, coach, healer, mentor, and even a shaman by some. Yet I do not claim to be a guru or spiritual master; I am an everyday person, just like you. I do feel compelled, however, to add two little points: I am now living an incredibly wonderful, abundant life; it is fun, and continually getting better. Also, I am a very special person; a very, very special person indeed.

Guess what. YOU ARE TOO! If you do not believe so right now, it's okay. Many, maybe even most of us learn not to think such thoughts about ourselves. In addition, when we feel broken or trapped in a behavioral, habitual, or physiological pattern, we cannot find a way to overcome, we do not feel very special. I know I certainly didn't, and I can tell you I encounter virtually the same sentiment in every new client I work with, at least at first, but usually not for long.

For instance, I recently worked with a lovely woman I'll call Angela, a 33-year-old stock broker and mother of two, who came to me with a lifelong history of general worry and social anxiety. She also described herself as an inveterate hypochondriac. Within a month, she had left all that behind, radiant in her new energy of confidence, self-control, and excellent health—a state of being that she now considers both normal and expected.

Or there's Henry, a 58-year-old business manager who in only two sessions found and connected to the inner resources he needed to lose 85 pounds—a kindness he wanted to bestow upon himself, but didn't think he could actually accomplish. Two sessions was all it took to get him on his way!

It is my hope that by the time we are through with our "session" together in these pages, you will have changed your mind completely about yourself. You will rediscover that you are a unique member of this club of ours called humanity, and in your uniqueness both incredibly special and completely deserving of having the life of your dreams become the life of your reality. I say *rediscover* because we all start out knowing that we are absolutely worthy and deserving of having anything we want; we're just trained almost from the very beginning of life to forget it. And so, because we are very little and don't know any better, we often do.

SYNTHESIS IS...

As a mixture of elements, Synthesis is partly composed of my personal philosophy, born of all my life experience combined with the knowledge acquired through all those years of research, studying and learning from some of the great minds in human development. Some of them you no doubt know and may have read or met, and some may be new to you. I will share a little of their teachings as they relate to Synthesis and also point you toward learning more from them if you so choose. I do so hope you choose to explore further, because there is a lot of great stuff out there.

Synthesis is, of course, also a product of what I have learned through my experience in clinical practice, working with more than 2,000 clients and seminar students from all lifestyles and professions, from age 7 to 85, and across the gamut of human behavior. I have been honored to assist so many wonderful people in transcending the common and sometimes not-so-common issues that held them in a paradigm of pain and brokenness. They, too, are just like you and me—normal, everyday, very special people. As with Angela and Henry, some of their stories are well worth sharing, so in these pages many will be.

It is important to add two points here: First, I purposely chose case histories that are both interesting and represent the full spectrum of issues I deal with repeatedly in literally thousands of cases and sessions—so anyone will likely see some of themselves and their issues in some of these stories. Second, my clients' trust, confidentiality, and privacy are absolutely sacrosanct, and thus I have changed certain details in all these cases so as to allow you, the reader, to recognize and understand the issue while at the same time ensuring that no individual client's privacy can or will be compromised. As they say in film dramas (even those based in fact), any resemblance to any person, living or dead, is purely coincidental.

I will give you a hint about something as well: In terms of wisdom or knowledge, there may be absolutely nothing new in this book. What we are discovering about our world and ourselves has always been there and known on some level since the dawn of civilization. Synthesis simply combines the old and new, and it strongly suggests a return to philosophical doctrines often derogatorily described as "woo-woo," or New Age, or metaphysical, and just as often verily tossed onto the junk heap of arcane nonsense by contemporary science and empirical thinkers. And surprise, surprise: the evidence that suggests that we return to and closely reexamine these precepts is all backed by hard, scientific evidence—yet more irony!

What can be—and I hope will be—new for you, however, is how it is all presented. Indeed, I have found that perception, perspective, and presentation is unique to each presenter, each teacher. A new and different perspective can hold the key to unlocking the gate to a marvelous and empowering adventure of understanding and personal growth that so many people seek, perhaps today more than ever.

For example, I am an avid golfer, and my wife often kids me about the fact that for years and years I have bought and continue to buy magazines, videos, books, and a myriad of training aids to help me understand and then execute a consistent and efficient golf swing. The golf swing itself is a simple yet complex, basic yet intricate athletic movement that hasn't changed that much in more than 700 years. Yet, it is subject to endless study, analysis, and interpretation, and a source of endless frustration for those who attempt it— that is, until they see, or read about, and then feel the swing from just the right perspective *for them*. With the right perspective, it becomes easy, and with a little practice it becomes consistently so.

Synthesis, too, is both simple and complex, and once understood and practiced consistently it becomes and stays easy! As I just wrote those words, I thought of Michelle, a would-be entrepreneur who first came to me stressed and figuratively paralyzed by an intense fear of failure. When she came in for her third session, she sat down and said, "I've been reading self-improvement books all my life, and never understood how it all really works until now."

After only six sessions, we said goodbye. She had just closed her first investment deal—something she was afraid she couldn't do—reporting that it felt as though it had almost fallen into her lap; from finding the right business to purchase, to securing the financing, just like that! Now fearless, empowered, and practicing Synthesis every day, as far as I can tell, she's well on her way to a wonderful and lucrative career and much more.

The consistent practice of Synthesis can also lead to a spectacular standard of living I like to call practical enlightenment. Practical enlightenment is itself a synthesis between the conscious and subconscious parts of the mind that creates a chain reaction of exponential empowerment; keeping ourselves growing, leading a life filled with love, abundance of any kind, and true peace of mind. This is a way of living that is very achievable by anyone willing to put in the effort. And oh, once you're there, it is so very worth it! I mean, who said we have to put a cap on happiness and personal growth? Is there a limit to how wonderful your life can become? To answer in one word: NO!

Synthesis provides a guide, a roadmap to make it as easy and as practical as possible. Perhaps it's best expressed by someone whose been through the process. Several months after we finished working together, Joseph, a contractor and single dad, wrote to say, "I am still doing the work that we started together; at times I am still quite surprised to realize how great I feel, both spiritually and physically. I am getting better at consistently choosing happiness and wellbeing; it has changed my life." That is what it's all about, so why not have that be you?

HOW TO USE THIS BOOK

As much as possible, I am going to introduce you to Synthesis very much the same way I do it in the clinic, or at a Synthesis seminar.

Take your time. There is a lot to think about and absorb; it is not meant to be accomplished in one sitting. As you will see, there is also much of what I call "chicken-and-egg-ness" going on. In real life all the ingredients, tools, and techniques of Synthesis happen at once, but in a book, they must be presented linearly, and often there is no clear logical order; any part can precede or follow any other. I ask your indulgence; at the end, I am confident that it will all make sense.

I have divided the book into three parts. Part I, "Foundations," sets the context for the rationale, models, and techniques of Synthesis. Before you can change anything about your life—big or small—you really need to understand who you are and how you got stuck; in other words, how and why you've come to think and behave the way you do. You have to look at and understand all the influences that made you, you.

First and foremost, *you* are a part of *us*, humanity. We are all, each of us, an amalgam, partly a product of our immediate environment and experiences, and partly a product of the evolution, history, development, and current state of our species, our culture, and our mass consciousness.

So, we'll begin setting context by taking a look at *us* through a brief and tiny little peek into some of the subjects I mentioned earlier—anthropology, history, and philosophy—as they relate to the state of our being and life in contemporary Western society. You will, I think, begin to see parts of yourself, your attitudes, and the roots of some (maybe all) of the issues that may be bothering you.

Then comes a little more context, a little physics, psychology, and some biology, looking at the nature of our world and the essence of universal reality and the human mind in terms of what we thought it was and what we are discovering it really is. I will introduce you to the discovery or rediscovery of the quantum or holographic model of universal structure and function, and we will briefly examine how that relates to the concept of life and what it means for you and how you live.

Trying to grasp and understand the idea of a quantum universe, "going down the rabbit hole," as it is described in the wonderful and highly recommended film on the subject, *What the Bleep Do We Know!?*, can be mind-blowing. Taken in bits, however, the scientific facts of it speak for themselves, and the model holds important and practical implications for each of us.

We'll examine what it means for *us* and for *you* to be defined as "quantum" or "holographic" beings, and what that suggests as to how our minds really work, how we view reality, and how we live our lives. As you will see, the potential generated by accepting ourselves as quantum beings in a quantum universe is enormous. Each of us can redefine the basis of our personal reality, a necessary precursor to creating change and personal growth. This may be eye-opening for you— it was for me, and it certainly is for most of my clients.

I am confident that the models, tools, and techniques of Synthesis as I understand and practice it will not only make perfect sense to you, but will also be easy and fun to use. And you will begin to use and practice Synthesis even as we set context. At the end of each chapter, I will provide summaries of key points and concepts, called "Takeaways"; important ideas that you might want to give more thought or even more research. (The Takeaways at the end of this

Introduction will incorporate some key points from the Preface as well.) I will also assign "Action Items." Action Items are activities to get you started and integrating Synthesis into your life right away, even as you are learning what it is, what it means, and how it works.

In Part II, "Getting to Know You," we will take this new view of universal reality and energy and frame it in practical terms, introducing you to *you* through what I call the models of Synthesis. You will meet yourself in terms of being a creator of your experiences and your reality. We'll explore the dynamics of the mind; we'll look at its components, structure, and functionality.

You'll see and understand how the mind develops, how we come to be who we are, and of course, how we get stuck in our issues and dis-eases, or what we'll be calling our energetic disconnections. We'll also discuss the concept of human beings as energetic entities; we'll see how the human energy system is constructed and operates. In other words, you will get to know yourself in a way that allows you to fully understand who you are and how and why you think and behave as you do.

In Part III, "From Theory to Practice—Creating a Better You," we bring it all together, putting all the theory behind Synthesis into a realistic methodology. I will present my recipe or formula for creating change of any kind in your life, explaining each ingredient in the formula, how it works, and how the ingredients need to come together to make your changes happen quickly and profoundly.

I will introduce you to the tools of Synthesis, and how we use them to work at both the conscious and subconscious levels of your mind. You will learn to tap into and utilize an inner power that for most Westerners has become almost vestigial—an ability that, once awakened, will never lead you astray. And you'll learn how the process of Synthesis evolves, with practice and refinement, from something at first very basic and perhaps somewhat awkward to a way of life that holds unlimited potential for continued personal growth.

Indeed, I will show you how you can use Synthesis to create that state of being I described earlier: practical enlightenment, a constant (or nearly so) state of awareness and mindfulness that enables an individual to actually live more powerfully, joyfully, and ecologically than most people today can even imagine. I assure you that living this way will make your life *a lot of fun*; it's a goal we all aspire to, even if sometimes unconsciously.

I've already mentioned this, but it is well worth repeating: Practical enlightenment is both attainable and worth attaining. To attain it is to not only supercharge your new life and your new future, but also to automatically become a transformer, a beacon of inspiration and hope to others, and, by default, a leader in the process of changing and healing our world. Please do not be frightened by that prospect. All you have to do is live your life the way you want to; the rest will happen naturally.

I firmly believe that the transformation and healing of mass consciousness must begin with individuals, people like you who are tired of the pain of living in disconnection, whatever that may be, and also brave enough to look past and transcend the dogma of an obsolete paradigm of thinking and living. These people will acknowledge and embrace what science is proving about the truth of the inner workings of nature and our world.

They will be bold enough to use that truth and take full and complete responsibility for, and then conscious control of how their lives unfold, and forever forego the role of victim. The clients I work with who succeed—and by far most of them do—go through this process, and usually do so very well. I believe you can and will too.

Again, we must begin by establishing at least a basic understanding of just how we got and get ourselves into our messes. There are two reasons to begin this way: First, each of us as an individual is reflective and part of *us* as a species, a culture, and a society. Second, to borrow an old truism, knowledge is power.

Think of your car, for example. Say you begin to hear a funny noise under the hood; the engine begins to run rough, or ping, or chug, or wheeze—or worse. If you know how the engine works, how the various systems come together to produce the power to drive the wheels, it's easier to dive in and repair it. Without that knowledge, fixing the engine would be much more difficult. Where would you start? What tools would you use? And even if you were handed the perfect set of tools for the job, how would you use them? Some might be quick to say, "No worries, I'll just take the car to a good mechanic and let him or her fix the engine." That might work for your car engine, because someone else can probably fix it, but only *you* can fix your life.

In Synthesis you will learn how your mind—the engine of behavior—works. You will be given a great set of tools. I will assist you in using them quickly and powerfully, but only you can do the actual work. So, let's get started. Who are we and how did we get here? Let's find out. Inquiring minds want to know!

INTRODUCTION SUMMARY
Takeaways

⇥ Rule #1: Life is supposed to be fun!

⇥ Much of the stress and overall disconnection we feel as individuals stems from isolation, a product of modern philosophy and Western culture.

⇥ Many individuals develop personal disconnection through succumbing to the wishes and expectations of others. They attempt to live in conflict with their core values. It is rarely feasible to do so and thrive for very long, if at all.

⇥ *You* are part of and reflective of *us*. Understanding how *we* got here will pave the way for understanding how *you* got here, and it will make the tools and process of Synthesis that much more powerful and effective.

⇥ Synthesis is a process; we establish context, present models and protocols to frame that context, and then practice and perfect the process to create any change you desire and more.

Action Items

⇥ Open your mind and your heart to insight and learning. Part of creating change requires objective assessment of your issue(s). As we explore our journey in the first chapter, you can (and I hope you will) begin to reflect upon your own journey.

⇥ Remember Tim, the law student? Ask yourself, *Am I living according to my core values, or someone else's?* If you cannot answer this question just yet, just let it remain an open question for now. The answer will come.

⇥ If possible, see if you can begin to consciously expect that you *will* indeed succeed in creating the change in your life you desire; at this point, any tiny bit of positive, conscious expectation is great. Go ahead, give yourself a little gift; begin to expect something to happen. Spend as little or as much time thinking about this as you wish, but the more the better. You may find it begins to create a little feeling of exhilaration and anticipation. This feeling is very, very good for you.

Part I

Foundations

Chapter 1:
Who Are We and How Did We Get Here?

Toto, I've a feeling we're not in Kansas anymore.
—Dorothy, *The Wizard of Oz*

I have always been fascinated by the mystery of our development and our evolution as a species. I'm especially curious about the enigma of just why and how we evolved as we did. Of all the creatures on Earth, why was it we who rose to dominance on the planet? To me, this question, like that of the human brain trying to figure itself out, is both somewhat ironic and profoundly interesting—and it may never be fully answered.

What we do know, of course, is that our great evolutionary advantage was our mind. Our brain. We developed the ability to think conceptually and abstractly, decipher cause and effect, and discover the how and why of things. This led to the appearance of social intelligence, or the ability to think and act as group, to cooperate in obtaining an outcome. Given that our early ancestors were much smaller and weaker than many of the critters they were trying to eat, this proved to be a huge advantage in ensuring our survival.

In and of itself, social intelligence is not unique to humans. But we took social intelligence to new levels, because we also developed complex language, which gave rise to what anthropologists call cultural evolution—an occurrence that *was* unique to our species, and, perhaps, the great differentiator between all our fellow creatures and us.

There was a huge chain of consequence from this development. We transcended the requirement for devoting all our time to simply ensuring survival; we got free time! With that time and our powerful, conceptual brains, we developed the ability to exert some control over our immediate environment. We learned to control fire, manufacture shelters, and make and use sophisticated tools. We learned to domesticate plants and animals, which led to settled, agricultural societies. We thus achieved an easier and relatively more comfortable existence, and with that came an awareness of subjective value, of duality, ease versus dis-ease, or what I call disconnection. More simply stated, we unwittingly invented the concept of contrast.

It is not a stretch to state that the essence of our further evolution hinged upon this single aspect: duality, contrast; more or less good or bad. Contrast makes possible the exclusively human concepts of ecstasy, love, passion, bliss, pleasure, health, wealth, and abundance, but these exquisite qualities of life have meaning only through the knowing of their opposites: agony, hate, apathy, misery, illness, poverty, and scarcity.

Contrast then, became (and remains) the single-most important factor through which we define and judge the human experience. It is our species' definitive and primordial meme. "Meme" comes from the Greek word *mimema*, meaning "something imitated." It is a term coined by evolutionary biologist Richard Dawkins, and refers to the concept of encoded and entrained thought patterns existing within and as part of a society's mass consciousness— the elements of their ethos.

Memes are considered to be almost like cultural genes that are automatically passed among individuals and from one generation to the next, and thus serve to both propagate and perpetuate cultural thought and behavioral patterns. The "science" of memes, called memetics, is considered unempirical, yet the idea that we pass on these so-called cultural genes among ourselves and between generations certainly seems to make sense when we look at how we live and behave.

With the invention or awareness of contrast—our primordial meme—the ship we might call modern humanity set sail, and the generation and development of the memes of modern mass consciousness began, all leading to who and why and how *we* and *you* live the way *we* and *you* do today. Contrast became and is both our greatest blessings and our greatest curse, because for some reason (and I believe we are unique in this regard as well) we have learned to be very tough on ourselves.

For instance, if a coyote hunting for his dinner sees and chases a rabbit, and that rabbit escapes, it is safe to assume that the coyote does not enter a deep funk or depression, or have an anxiety attack. He does not develop a rabbit phobia, or suffer a blow to his self-esteem. He does not chastise himself as he drinks himself into a stupor at the local Coyote tavern: "Oh dear, I am a bad coyote; I am unworthy; I do not even deserve a rabbit; I am depressed; I am a disgrace to coyote-dom!" No, he just gets right back to hunting and keeps at it until he finds a slower rabbit.

Only we engage in such self-judgment and self-degradation—"I'm not cool enough, smart enough, sexy enough, rich enough, brave enough, lovable enough, whatever enough. I'm not worthy. I'm less than. I'm a failure." And we do it quite well! Do you see any of your current feelings about yourself, your behaviors, or your life in those statements?

I bet I know the answer. I *never ever* receive calls from people who are suffering from too much happiness, abundance, comfort, control, or peace of mind in their lives. None of my clients calls and asks, "Doctor John, can I come in for a few sessions? I'm feeling way too good."

On the contrary, I only hear from people who are in a state of disconnection and want something they do not have, or want to get rid of something they do have. Either way, their "something" is always triggered through a feeling of lack, of being less than, unworthy, or a failure in some way. And it almost always stems at least in part from comparing themselves to some arbitrary societal or cultural standard(s)—some meme—as to what is enough, or cool, or acceptable.

As we evolved and advanced, as we gained even more comfort and more free time, we came to want more of it. We consequently also became more and more curious about the bigger picture. We began to want to understand the big and sometimes scary world in which we live and also more about our place within that world, both in terms of our existence on earth and within the greater context of the cosmos, the universe. Why? Again, we turn to contrast. The more we learned, the more we felt in control of our existence. The less mysterious the world felt, the greater our comfort level living in it.

At the 1988 Scientific Symposium, Travis W. Binion stated in a keynote address that human cognition and curiosity manifested in three main forms of endeavor: religion, science, and philosophy. "Religion delves into the spiritual realm, science into the physical realm, and philosophy unifies the two in a pervasive search for universal reality," he said.[1] He also asserted that these three disciplines became innate to the human condition, and the anthropological evidence supports this idea. All ancient cultures and civilizations produced and practiced some form of religion, explored science, and generated philosophical theories and doctrines.

"So, who cares? What's the big deal?" you might ask. Well for me, the big deal is that despite differences in specific traditions, ceremonies, and religious practices—what we might call cultural semantics—and despite being separated by vast geographic barriers and distances, the worldviews of the early indigenous cultures regarding the structure and function of the universe and their place and role within it were uncannily similar.

As illustrated earlier by the story of Pigeon Feather and Little Quill, the societies and cultures of the native peoples around the globe were defined by community, energetic connection, and contiguity: oneness and balance between and among all things and all beings throughout the tribe and throughout existence. This way of life is often referred to as "the old ways" by descendents of these peoples. This is a point worth examining a bit further.

My search of the literature revealed virtually no mention of mental illness among indigenous peoples—that is, at least *before* they were exposed to Western culture. In other words, when living by the old ways, the people of native societies did not seem to suffer endemic low self-esteem, chronic worry, or chronic stress. They did not seem to experience anxiety disorders, panic attacks, or phobias. They apparently also felt no need to numb themselves from the realities of life with drugs or alcohol or other behavioral addictions. They did not appear to suffer from depression, mood swings, social anxiety, obsessive-compulsive disorder, ADD, binge eating, mass anger, or any of the other of the myriad and all too pervasive disconnections that are endemic to us in contemporary society. Interesting.

Did they know something we don't? Seems so. We might infer that living in connection, community, and unity as they did was beneficial to the health and wellbeing of both the individual and the tribe. We might also infer that these people somehow avoided succumbing to the meme and disconnection of chronic lack. Surely, as "modern humans" they understood duality and contrast; they simply and clearly handled it differently.

I believe it is because they lived in energetic balance among themselves and with the world around them. I also believe that it was losing this connection and balance that helped spawn the great social and individual disconnection we live with and suffer under in modern society.

Indeed, as our modern Western societies developed we left the old ways far behind. The more we learned and the less mysterious the world felt to us, the greater our comfort level and sense of control, and the more powerful we felt. The more comfort, control, and power we felt, the more comfort, control, and power we wanted; and, ironically, the more we also realized how little of those attributes were actually in hand. Yet more lack!

And on it went; our incessant craving for greater control and comfort in turn generated increasing isolation from both the natural world and our sense of community with one another and our fellow creatures.

Isolation and separateness are two of the core concepts imbued into all Western thought as expressed through those common and innate activities of religion, science, and philosophy. And to me they appear to be the breeding ground of many (if not most) of the social pathogens that plague our society. Ours is a philosophy that separates the individual from the community, destroys the concept of unity and connection, and has spawned a culture burdened and sickened by contrast and a seemingly constant sense of lack.

We have become a species lost in a world of artifice and the virtual rather than grounded in the real: video games, online relationships, television, movies, and voiceless communication consume enormous amounts of our time and attention. Our incessant desire for instant everything—including physical and emotional gratification, success, and our seemingly limitless hunger for acquiring more things and even more free time—has become apparently essential to our way of life. This way of life has created enormous disconnection. This is who we are today.

But how did we get here? It was, quite simply, a result of our getting even smarter and inventing modern science and philosophy.

MODERN SCIENCE AND PHILOSOPHY

It is generally accepted that modern philosophical/scientific thought owes its existence to the ancient Greeks, who actually invented the very idea of philosophy—pursuing knowledge for the sake of knowledge itself. The great Greek thinkers transcended the belief of a world controlled by mythical gods and goddesses, to conceive the idea that the universe was a kind of machine subject to rigid laws.

Aristotle, a student of Plato and one of the most famous of the ancient Greek philosophers, created a theory of universal structure based upon the idea of a hierarchy. In his model, everything in existence was ranked, from the "impermanent" creatures of Earth to the "permanent" heavenly bodies moving in eternal motion and controlled by God.

This hierarchical model of nature was later adopted by many Christian, Jewish, and Muslim theologians in the Middle Ages. Once religion assimilated a hierarchical, God-controlled system of nature's order and function, it assimilated science itself. "Science equals religion" became the core premise of a belief system that significantly clouded (and at times even forbade) rational thinking. This doctrine greatly impeded both scientific and philosophic exploration and progress well into the 16th century.

Fortunately, in 1543, Nicolaus Copernicus drove what has been termed the first stake into the heart of this dogma with his manuscript *De revolutionibus orbium coelestium*, or *On the Revolution of Heavenly Spheres*. This seminal work essentially debunked the then-accepted and Church-supported notion that the Earth was the center of the universe. Indeed, Copernicus's work is sometimes described as the trigger of the Scientific Revolution, a movement that would usher in a new worldview.

The Renaissance and Great Enlightenment were times of great upheaval and change. Science became a quest for uncovering and understanding the natural world based upon solid fact and experimental evidence. In Italy, physicist and astronomer Galileo Galilei was of great importance to furthering this wave of new thinking. He created the science of mechanics, which applied the principles of geometry to the motions of bodies. The success of mechanics in discovering apparently reliable and useful laws of nature suggested a central premise: that all of nature is designed in accordance with mechanical laws.

In 1619, French philosopher and mathematician Rene Descartes set down four rules for applying his method for finding "truth," the most important of which was: Never accept anything as true or real which is not clearly *known to be true.* Descartes was also one of the first modern thinkers to consider the mind and body as separate and distinct, a model of thought called dualism. The body was considered akin to a machine that operated under the laws of physics. The mind—separate, invisible, and an ethereal entity—was therefore not subject to these same laws.

This concept of a mechanistic world consisting of independent bodies and systems that can and may interact with one another, but that are and always remain separate, continued to evolve to become the very core of Western philosophy and scientific method. Later, the work of Sir Isaac Newton, inarguably one of the greatest minds in human history, assured its permanence.

Newton's laws of motion confirmed many of Galileo's discoveries, and led directly to the development of contemporary or modern physics. Newton's model presented the elements and systems of the universe as divisible and wholly self-contained. His was a material world in which particles of matter follow certain laws of motion through both space and time. In other words, with Newtonian physics, the universe was officially defined as a big machine and "I'll believe it when I see it" became the official mantra of Western scientific method and thought.

Much later, in 1859, but following the by now well-established model of Newtonian, mechanistic science, Charles Darwin's theory of Natural Selection further cemented the notion of duality, separation, and isolation. Evolution through natural selection emphasizes separation and competition between and among species and biological systems. Thus, it not only fit in with but also strengthened the apparent veracity of the Newtonian model of nature as a collection of independent mechanistic systems—a paradigm that remains the mainstream view today.

THE GREAT SEPARATION

In terms of the advancement of knowledge, splitting science from religion was a major and necessary step forward; however, in doing so, we also inadvertently rejected the connection between the realms of the physical and the *spiritual.* It was an understandable but costly consequence, what I call the Great Separation.

In the days of Copernicus, spirituality and religion were considered synonymous; a misguided idea that still exists in many parts of society to this day. However, we must remember an important distinction: Religion is man-made; spirit—the essence of life itself—is not. Nonetheless, as science continued to evolve beyond religion, the requirement to stay independent of anything smacking of the intangible or metaphysical became paramount. The modern scientific paradigm became one of absolute mechanistic empiricism: Accept as science only that information supported by solid evidence and fact. Thus, the Great Separation proliferated into every area of mainstream thought.

That this occurred is even more understandable when we consider that as a direct result of this change in thinking, the modern sciences of physics, chemistry, biology, and so on, have allowed us to *seemingly* decipher many of the apparent mechanisms of the natural world, including ourselves. Moreover, no rational person would likely decry the fact that the technologies developed under the aegis of Western philosophy and science have, in many ways, proffered a better quality of life for most people and on many levels.

We can fly around the globe at incredible speeds. We can communicate with virtually anyone, at any time, from anywhere, and obtain information and images instantly. We have been to the moon and back. For most of us, not only the necessities but also many of the so-called luxuries of life are right at our fingertips. Further, who doesn't know someone whose life was saved by modern science and medical protocols? If you know or are one of those people, as I am, you are very, very grateful for modern medical technology and protocols. So on and on it goes, and at a high level, it all looks good. Yeah, but. But, what?

But, as a result of all this, the metaphysical concept of spiritual energy, of Oneness—connection between and among all things, including man and the natural world on Earth and the greater universe beyond—was discarded, summarily tossed into the philosophical junk heap of the arcane and esoteric and then virtually lost to ensuing generations. We are today almost completely isolated from an integral part of our very essence, our spirit or Source Energy.

In his wonderfully readable and cogently written *The Divine Matrix*, author Gregg Braden quotes a Native American wisdom keeper in summarizing how the Great Separation occurred. I love this passage, as it seems to convey the tale perfectly:

A long time ago, our world was very different from the way we see it today. There were fewer people, and we lived closer to the land. People knew the language of the rain, the crops, and the Great Creator. They even knew how to speak to the stars and the sky people. They were aware that life is sacred and comes from the marriage between Mother Earth and Father Sky. In this time there was balance and people were happy... Then something happened. No one really knows why but the people started forgetting who they were. In their forgetting they began to feel separate—separate from the earth, from each other, even from the one who created them. They were lost and wandered through life with no direction of connection. On their separation, they believed that they had to fight to survive in this world and defend themselves against the same forces that gave them the life they had learned to live in harmony with and trust. Soon all of their energy was used to protect themselves from the world around them, instead of making peace with the world within them... Even though they had forgotten who they were, somewhere inside of them the gift of their ancestors remained...they knew they held the power to heal their bodies, bring rain when they needed to, and speak with their ancestors... As they tried to remember who they were, they began to build things *outside* of their bodies that reminded them of who they were on the *inside*. They even built machines to do their healing, made chemicals to grow their crops, and stretched wires to communicate over long distances. The farther they wandered from their inner power, the more cluttered their outer lives became with the things they believed would make them happy.[2]

Through the Great Separation, we have come to suffer greatly. Dr. Bruce Lipton asserts, "When science turned away from spirit, its mission dramatically changed."[3] That change was drastic. Modern science embarked on a mission of giving humanity control and domination over nature rather than attempting to better understand how we can live in harmony with and within it. This in turn unleashed a rampage of egoism that became and remains ravenous.

Instead of life being about an empowered *me* helping all of *us*, it's now about *me* for *me* alone. In addition, the notion of *me*, *me*, and more *me* bred and breeds greed, selfishness, prejudice, isolation, and the insatiable urge to control and dominate even more—both the world in which we live and those with whom we share it.

The more comfort and ease the ego gets, the more it wants, and the less it is willing to do in order to get what it wants; it comes to feel entitled. *Entitled* is a far, far different notion than *deserving*, as we will discuss later on. As a result, we have done and continue to do great harm to our species, our fellow creatures, and the planet itself. Can we heal and reintegrate?

The prevailing opinion of experts and spiritual masters regarding the answer to this question appears to lean firmly toward the affirmative. We can heal and reintegrate, and to do so we are advised to take a look back to the tribal cultures, to the old ways. The central theme or tenet of the old ways of *energetic balance and spiritual connection* defined a reality that seemed to work quite well.

The old ways were also reflective of a way of thinking that was diametrically opposed to that of contemporary Western philosophy. This was wonderfully described by one of the great shamans of the Sioux nation, Frank Fools Crow, who said, "It is absolutely fundamental that we must believe in order to see, rather than to follow the scientific approach of seeing in order to believe."[4] Dr. Lipton mirrors this view—as do many other experts—when he states, "Never have we needed the insights of such a world view more."[5]

Yet, we must also acknowledge that we cannot change the way our mass consciousness works or thinks in a thrice. We remain burdened with centuries of encoding and entrainment in the Newtonian-Darwinian worldview, exemplified by what I call the *Seven Deadly Memes of modern culture*:

1. Obsession with lack
2. Incessant desire for control and comfort
3. Isolation
4. The Great Separation
5. Excessive empiricism
6. Conditional love
7. Falsely (externally) derived self-esteem—basing our sense of worth on the opinion/s of others

These Seven Deadly Memes, a somewhat tongue-in-cheek parallel to the infamous seven deadly sins, are, like their counterparts, largely ego-driven, and I think reflective of our mass consciousness. They emerged in parallel with, and as a result of, the development of modern culture, science, and philosophy, all beginning with our original and primordial meme—the notion of contrast. They appeared somewhat sequentially, yet once formed, and now well established, they simultaneously feed off and perpetuate one another in an unending cycle of destructive and debilitating energy (See Figure 1).

Figure I

The Seven Deadly Memes

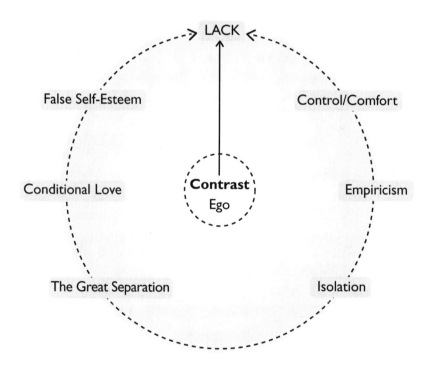

THE POWER OF MASS CONSCIOUSNESS

As mentioned earlier, the science of memetics is considered unempirical, yet it is clear that we are all exposed to the energy of these memes of mass consciousness on a daily basis. We are literally bombarded with their energy on and from all sides—both within our immediate environment, and from outside—basically from the time we are born. This phenomenon is also, at least in part, the source of most everyone's disconnection. I'd like to share a couple of examples, one from my own life and one from a recent client case.

For a good portion of my life, I was pretty insecure; in some ways extremely so. Where did that come from? Well, growing up in the 1950s and early 60s, the days of increasing escalation in the Cold War between the United States and the Soviet Union, the threat of nuclear war was palpable. I vividly remember having regular air raid drills in grade school. The alarm would go off and we'd all be hustled down to the basement of the school to the so-called fallout shelter. I can remember yellow and black radiation warning signs posted all over town, providing directions to public bomb shelters.

Every Saturday at around 12 o'clock or so all the towns and cities in the area would test the civil defense system. Air raid sirens would all go off and howl for about five minutes, and it seemed to my young mind as if everything and everyone stopped what they were doing and blankly stared at the sky until the sirens stopped; as if they were waiting for something. But for what?

I also remember routinely seeing lots of military planes flying overhead as well, and it seemed that on the news every night was a constant chatter about the rising risk of nuclear war and annihilation. It *seemed* as if all the adults in the world spoke of nothing but the Soviet threat. I was about 6 or 7 when all this began, and I was terrified, sure that at any minute, I—we—would all be vaporized and die a horrible death.

That feeling of utter helplessness worsened as, right in the middle of all this, my parents filed for divorce. As a result I learned to be afraid of virtually everything—carnival rides, ski lifts, horror movies, even the dark; anything that was out of my control, which seemed like everything. I lived every day with a constant sense of smoldering dread that could be fanned into terror in an instant. That dread evolved into basic insecurity, one of the taproots of my disconnection, before I learned Synthesis and how to take control of my life.

The Cold War is over, but it seems that there is always some pervading negative energy in our mass consciousness, which permeates our immediate surroundings and instills fear, uncertainty, and pessimism, as I witnessed in working with one of my clients not long ago.

Janine, is a fine artist in her early 30s who came to me for help in changing what she described as a generally unhappy, generally negative, and cynical attitude toward herself and her life. It was a self-assessment with which I could not disagree when very early in our first session she animatedly stated, "I mean, like, what's the use? Just look at the world out there; it sucks; it's all going to hell! I sometimes wonder, what's the point of even living?"

You can just imagine how she reacted to hearing me state just a few moments later that I absolutely believe life is supposed to be fun and that soon I both hoped and expected she would agree with me. We clearly had some work to do.

Once we began working together, I quickly discovered that she basically had inherited her negative outlook from her parents, particularly her dad, with whom, when growing up, she had routinely watched the news while eating dinner.

Mass media is a huge creator, reflector, and perpetuator of memes and mass consciousness, focusing almost exclusively on what's wrong in our world—on lack and negativity. As Janine related, nightly and for years they would watch and listen, and her dad would editorialize—grumbling and complaining about the horrible state of the world and the people in it. Apparently, her dad sincerely believed that people with positive attitudes were all a put-on. He described them as "A bunch of $&#@ Mary Poppinses," and on the rare occasion that a positive story was reported, he would typically rail at the tube, then wink at her and say, "We're too smart to be taken in by that crap, aren't we?"

Janine's current boyfriend apparently shared similar views. He had actually tried to convince her not to work with me because, like her dad, he believed that happy, empowered people are simply faking it. I quickly assured her—*and I assure you*—they are not!

I have had many clients cave in to the negativity of friends, family, and/or loved ones and quit before they made their breakthrough, but Janine somehow resisted and continued to come back. She responded well to hypnosis, which creates an open, flexible, and receptive state of mind (what we might call a learning state), and she was diligent in doing her daily reinforcement homework. She progressed quickly.

At the outset of our fourth session, I asked her how she was feeling. Her face lit up. She reported feeling "great," and added that she had just been commissioned that day to paint a mural for a major corporation's new headquarters and for a very lucrative sum. "Excellent," I answered. "What else?"

She paused a moment and then I watched her smile evaporate as quickly as it had appeared, replaced by an expression reminiscent of the dour and sullen look I'd seen on day one. She related that, as good as she felt, she was also experiencing a fair amount of friction in her relationship. Her boyfriend could not abide her new positive outlook and attitude. When that morning she had received the call for the audition and then wondered aloud if it could be related to her improving optimism, he had sneered and said, "Come on honey, you're much too smart to get fooled by that nonsense."

I was ready with a very quick response.

"Does that sound familiar?"

"Oh, yeah," she said. "I recognized it right away; I'm dating my dad."

"Okay, now let me ask you, which feels better to you: the way you feel now, or the way you felt when you first came in a few weeks ago?"

"The way I feel now."

"Okay, good. Now tell me, are you faking it?"

"No! I've genuinely been feeling really good, and really optimistic. I've been feeling almost lighter in a way."

"Great, so you can choose who you want to believe: yourself and how you feel, or the naysayers who think you're faking it or being fooled. And it is your choice of course."

※ ※ ※

Both my experience and Janine's case are perfect examples of just how affected we are by the people around us and the energy of the memes of mass consciousness, which can and do affect entire populations. Behavioral scientists call this mass contagion. This phenomenon of mass contagion gives new significance to the concept of peer pressure. And again, if we consider just how small the world we live in has become, given the existence of high-speed travel and instantaneous global communications, the idea of the mass contagion of the seven deadly memes takes on entirely new dimensions. How can you and we overcome this?

FINDING OUR WAY TO RECONNECTION

In order to change our worldview, to return to a philosophy of community and personal empowerment for the sake of both the individual and the greater good, to reestablish connection and balance between the physical and spiritual, we must change the way we think as individuals, and also form new "tribes" of like-minded individuals. That will help form and facilitate new memes into our mass consciousness, which will then create a new social contagion of unity and connection. Great, but that sounds so pie-in-the-sky, doesn't it? Just how do we do that?

Well, because the typical contemporary Western mind operates according to the Newtonian-Darwinian model ("I'll believe it when I see it"), I believe that the very best way to accelerate the formation and cultural embrace of these new memes is through the aegis of rigorous, empirical science—ironically, the very model of thought that got us lost to begin with.

To do this, we would need to find some scientific proof that there is a necessary and real connection between the physical and spiritual in the natural order of things. We would need to show that to acknowledge and embrace this connection could help us to create or re-create a healthy species and a healthy world reality. And here comes some very good news.

That scientific proof is surfacing daily and around the globe, through what can only be described as astounding discoveries in the intriguing science of quantum physics, quantum field theory, and in related disciplines such as epigenetics and neurophysiology.

Quantum mechanics represents cutting-edge science that simultaneously explores and seeks to understand the very essence of the universe at the infinitesimal and infinite levels, to uncover and explain the fundamental nature of nature, of all that exists, and in so doing, perhaps uncover the very character of creation itself.

Quantum theory was first formulated and introduced in 1900 by a physicist named Max Planck who was studying the nature of energy change in thermal radiation. According to MIT physicists Daniel Kleppner and Roman Jackiw, quantum mechanics, born of Planck's initial research "...was created to describe an abstract world far removed from daily experience, [yet] its impact on our daily lives could hardly be greater."[6] How great is that impact? Pretty great!

Drs. Kleppner and Jackiw state that many (if not most) of the major discoveries and developments in the modern sciences—chemistry, biology, medicine, and so on—as well as advances in the fields of electronics and photonics that gave rise to the Computer Age, the Information Age, and our global economy, owe their existence to the tools provided by quantum mechanics: "The creation of quantum physics has transformed our world, bringing with it all the benefits—and the risks—of [another] scientific revolution."[7]

They go on to say, "Quantum theory is the most precisely tested and most successful theory in the history of science. Yet it was deeply disturbing to its founders and remains so today, 75 years after it took its current form."[8] It is in fact so deeply disturbing that conventional science has so far simply chosen to ignore much of it.

Why would that be? Metaphorically stated, quantum physics, and perhaps more so quantum field theory, can be likened to a Force 5 hurricane that is wreaking havoc on the formerly calm and tranquil seas of more than 450 years of traditional Western scientific (Newtonian-Darwinian) thinking. And therein lays the big rub! When taken past what might be termed the practical applications and developments in conventional science and technology, discoveries in this vast, complex subject are rocking the Newtonian-Darwinian scientific model's boat—and rocking it very, very hard.

Quantum research is uncovering new ground that strongly suggests we *must* reconsider the way not only the universe, but also the creatures in it (including ourselves) work; that our contemporary world view is at the very least incomplete, and, much more likely, fundamentally inaccurate. And that is uncomfortable for scientists, because they thought they had it pretty much all figured out! As writer Michael Talbot observed, "Science is not always as objective as we would like to believe. We view scientists with a bit of awe, and when they tell us something, we are convinced it must be true. We forget they are human and subject to the same religious, philosophical, and cultural prejudices as the rest of us."[9]

Yale University surgeon Bernie Siegel, as quoted by Talbot, said it even more simply: "People are addicted to their beliefs."[10] And we have believed Newton and Darwin for a very long time.

Stated another way, the traditional models that seemed to work so well for so long are familiar, comfortable, and known, and thus have become ingrained and automatic—memes. People will hold onto the familiar with tenacity, even when the familiar is painful, limiting, or clearly self-sabotaging. This characteristic or tendency is known as homeostasis.

Homeostasis is a term derived from new Latin: *homeo,* "the same"; *stasis,* "state"—thus "same state." It is the inertia of homeostasis created by an innate fear of change that keeps people (scientists or not) stuck in their behavioral, emotional, and habitual patterns. Breaking homeostasis is actually one of the key prerequisites for all personal growth and change. (We will examine the development and effects of homeostasis in more depth a little later.)

米 米 米

So, now we know who *we* are and how *we* got here. And now you have a bit more insight into who *you* are and how *you* got here from the big-picture perspective. As I mentioned, there is more to do in regard to having you completely understand *you,* and we'll get to it in just a bit, but first comes the next step in setting context and foundations for Synthesis. That step is to take a peek into the maelstrom, right into the eye of the hurricane: the wonderful and mysterious domain of quantum theory. T.S. Eliot once wrote, "Human beings cannot stand too much reality." I completely disagree.

Let's see just what the fuss is all about. By examining just a few of the key discoveries in quantum science, you will see firsthand how accepting a quantum reality can and will help us change how *you* and *we* think about the world and *your/our* place within it. In doing so, we will begin to assemble the tools to reweave the fabric of *your/our* existence, undo the Great Separation and the effects of the other seven deadly memes—something that must happen if *you* are to live the life you dream of, and if *we* are to save ourselves.

CHAPTER 1 SUMMARY
Takeaways

⇥ Human social and cultural evolution resulted in our recognizing the notion of subjective value—contrast—which became and remains the basis of our entire existence.

⇥ As modern societies, science, and philosophy developed, we began to fathom and believe in the functionality of the universe and nature as a huge machine to be formulized and manipulated. We began to consider and believe ourselves to be both separate from the natural world and capable of controlling it to suit our fancy; we lost the concept of spirit and energetic connection.

⇥ As we separated and isolated ourselves, we also succumbed to the vicissitudes of rampant ego and our obsession with lack, and this has manifested in modern society's suffering from endemic disconnection.

⇥ Arising from contrast, the seven deadly memes of mass consciousness are:

- Obsession with lack
- Craving control and dominance
- Personal and societal isolation
- Empiricism ("I'll believe it when I see it.")
- The Great Separation of the physical and spiritual realms
- Conditional love
- Falsely derived (externally driven) self-esteem

⇥ Native tribal cultures seemed to suffer much less emotional and behavioral disconnection than we do. The old ways of defining reality and our place within the world may help show the way out of our endemic disconnection.

⇥ Quantum mechanics, a product of Western science, is ironically showing us that the conventional model of Western Science—based upon isolation and separateness—is severely limited and apparently quite inaccurate.

Action Items

⇥ Review and examine the seven deadly memes. Do you see any of yourself—your disconnection—reflected in them? Simply take note of this for now.

⇥ Open up to the possibility of finding your "tribe"; a feeling of a supportive, cooperative, connected community. Do not worry or give any thought to where it will come from or how big it will be; simply be open to finding it.

⫞ Once or twice a day—preferably twice—and *every day*, find a place, indoors or outside, where you can sit quietly, *without distraction or disturbance*. Close your eyes and take 21 slow, deep, gentle breaths. *Take your time*, and count them. If you lose count, start over. (You almost certainly will lose count. It's okay, just keep at it.) When you successfully reach 21 breaths, you're done. That's all.

⫞ Continue to be mindful of and working on the action items from the Introduction.

Chapter 2:
Looking Through the Looking Glass

To Infinity and Beyond!
—Buzz Lightyear

What is reality? It's a very big question; one that I suppose can have many answers. For example, as we have already discussed, we, humanity, have evolved and developed into what we are today; we have our current forms of culture and society, science and technology, philosophies and religions, the seven deadly memes, and so on, and all this clearly helps define our existence and our reality. We are a reflection of our history.

But let's look a little deeper, behind and through the reflection in the looking glass. What is reality for you or me as an individual? My answer is that our reality is what we are experiencing and feeling on two levels: There is the reality of any given moment, and a more general reality in terms of how we are feeling about our lives. I suppose we could also say that the realities of our individual living moments progressively occurring one after another sort of line up and combine to create the more general reality of our life. For example, if you are generally feeling productive, fulfilled, happy, and peaceful, that is your reality. But if you are generally feeling disconnection, which could manifest as feeling angry, sad, fearful, isolated, or in some other way broken, then that is your reality.

Okay, fine, that all seems simple enough, but I think we need to dig even deeper and ask an even more interesting question: How does reality occur? Where does our reality come from? Does it just happen, or do we have something to do with it? Here is the answer: No, reality does not just happen to us; we create it—good or bad, happy or sad. We create our own reality. It may not feel that way, but like it or not, that seems to be the case.

When I introduce this idea to a new client, I often get a lively response, something such as, "How can that be? I would never purposely do this to myself, create a reality of disconnection that is so painful, or frustrating, or unhappy, or addictive. What about the seven deadly memes you just told me about? You're actually suggesting that *I did this?*"

"Sorry," I say to them and to you, "like it or not, you did and do create your reality." Is your reality reflective of the strengths and foibles of your parents, friends, loved ones, acquaintances, and mass consciousness—deadly memes and all? Sure, partly. We use the database of the sum of our experiences, and our experiences are a product of all of the above. (We will look into the mechanism of all this a bit later.)

As for answering the "how can that be" part of the question, and also resolving what may appear to be a large contradiction based upon where we've been so far, we must now turn to the cutting-edge and astounding realm of quantum science.

QUANTUM SCIENCE

Science seeks truth; it always has. Of course, what appears true in one era often changes: what was science fiction becomes science, and what was conjecture or theory becomes fact. For instance, at one time, pretty much everyone on the planet believed the Earth was flat, and that humans could never fly, much less travel to outer space and safely return. Who could conceive that we would someday be able to view events half a world away, live and in HD?

In the same vein, up through about the turn of the last century or so, it was generally accepted that no piece of matter smaller than an atom could exist. We now know that is not the case: There are many smaller bits of matter and energy called subatomic particles. Scientists can now actually isolate and study a single unit of light energy (a photon) or a single unit of electricity (an electron). And there are even smaller particles than these currently under study. This is the realm of quantum physics and quantum mechanics, the study and exploration to discover the very essence of our universe; the search to understand the ultimate reality of our existence.

In 1905, not long after Max Planck initially formulated his theory of quanta or discrete levels of vibrational energy, other experimental physicists discovered that photons, the elemental components of light, can and do actually take two physical forms. They can manifest either as distinct particles, or as a continuum or wave. Whereas that at first seemed a bit odd, far more puzzling was the seemingly concurrent discovery that photons would also consistently exhibit whichever of the two states a given experimenter was *looking for or expecting to see* in a given experiment!

It was also soon discovered that, similar to photons, electrons are also not simply little bits or particles. In fact, an electron will always display the properties of a wave *until it is observed*, at which time it will take form and manifest as a discrete thing or particle. Scientists had discovered that the thoughts and/ or observations—in other words, participation—of the experimenter actually affects the nature or form of the energy, and therefore the outcome of the experiment.

Further research revealed that atoms are also not discrete "things" at all, but merely energetic "tendencies" waiting to manifest. Thus, instead of a teeny little solar system of discrete particles or objects, protons and neutrons orbited by electrons (the Newtonian view), an atom is really more like a fuzzy, blurry cloud of energy that comes into focus and becomes real or solid only when it is observed.

Think of a hummingbird's wings as it hovers at a flower; they are a blur of moving energy. With a high-speed camera, we can freeze the motion and see the actual structure of the wings. Similarly, when we observe an atom, it's like taking a high-speed photograph, except that the atom literally changes itself from a "tendency" into something discrete or solid.

What this means, of course, is that in the very act of observing, the observer has a profound and direct effect on the basic nature and structure of the atom, the smallest elemental building block of all matter. Another way of expressing this might be to say that through the interaction of observing, the observer "creates" the instantaneous physical reality or structure of the atom;

thus, and again, we see that the energy of thought affects the physical state and energy of matter itself!

Later, scientists also discovered that this behavior, the ability to switch forms from particle to wave and back, is common to all subatomic particles—light, radiation, radio waves, and so on—and here it gets even more bizarre. It turns out that different forms of energy are able to not only change form, but also change identity. For instance, an electron can transform into a proton and back again. This discovery clearly threw a proverbial monkey wrench (ouch!) into the Newtonian model of a mechanistic world filled with discrete bodies and systems. But wait—as they say in the infomercials—there's more!

Some 40 years after these initial discoveries, physicist Dr. David Bohm's work on plasma at the University of California's Lawrence Radiation laboratory revealed an even more peculiar phenomenon, and in doing so unveiled another key component of quantum mechanics now known as quantum field theory. Bohm discovered that once electrons were in a plasma—a gas containing a high density of electrons and positive ions—they stopped behaving as individuals and instead began to act as if they were part of an interconnected whole, "as if they were organized according to an almost intelligent design."[1] He called this phenomenon "interconnectedness."

Interconnectedness, also known as quantum entanglement, in essence suggested that subatomic particles and all matter are actually connected through a subtle field of energy. Bohm described this as the field of quantum potential. This was a disturbing notion to some physicists. Its effects were observed and verified in experiment after experiment, yet it could not actually be detected and measured.

One of the most famous of such experiments involved photons and polarizing screens. A polarizing screen is an apparatus that will deflect any light energy that strikes it in one of two possible random directions. In this experiment, scientists split a photon in two, creating identical twin photons, and then simultaneously fired or projected the twins at two different polarizing screens. With two possible paths of travel, the now independent photons were expected to behave randomly, each going one way or the other on a 50-50 basis, sort of like flipping a coin.

But this random behavior *never* occurred. Regardless of how many times the experiment was repeated, and even when they were separated by vast distances (thousands of miles), the twin photons *always* behaved the same way at the same instant in time when fired at their respective screens. They *always deflected in the same direction*, as if they were still somehow connected to one another and perhaps in some way even communicating.

This phenomenon clearly alluded to the veracity of Bohm's belief in the interconnectedness of all matter through the field of quantum potential. It was termed and became known as non-locality. Many scientists, including Albert Einstein, were never comfortable with quantum field theory primarily because of non-locality, which, although repeatedly observed and verified, simply could not be explained. Einstein is famous for his description of the phenomenon as "spooky action at a distance."

To add more fuel to the proverbial fire, it was also known that in any experiment involving quantum particles, there is always a tiny but constant mathematical anomaly present that equated to an infinitesimal bit of residual energy. This energetic anomaly was sort of like finding a tiny remainder in a long division problem, even when dividing even numbers. If this energy in fact existed, it would correspond nicely to Bohm's theory of a subtle field of quantum potential connecting all space and matter. However, at the time, the technology to actually detect and measure it did not exist. So, because they couldn't actually detect it, scientists at the time simply factored it into their calculations as if it was not there.

Today science does have the capability to detect and measure Bohm's field of quantum potential. It is miniscule in force at any given point in space, but the field exists and is reflective of a subtle but continuous exchange of energy between subatomic particles. It is an energy field that in effect fills the void or space between things. Of course, that means there actually *is no void between things*. There is no empty space—everything is connected through, by, and to this energy.

In essence, then, quantum science is proving through rigorous scientific experimentation that our world, our universe, is composed of one thing and one thing only: energy. We can picture it—the universe—as one massive, infinite field or matrix of energy, something like a giant spider web. Everything that exists is part of it, connected to it, and interconnected to everything else within it. Another way of describing this phenomenon is to liken the universe to a hologram, which is an image in which all the constituent parts contain a copy of the whole.

This "holographic" image or energy pattern is one we can see repeated throughout nature, such as in a flock of birds or a school of fish. These groups comprise many individuals that together act and behave as if they are a single organism, moving in absolute unison and acting as a connected group, in so doing helping to ensure the survival of the individuals, the flock or school, and of course the species itself. It seems logical to conclude that it is the connecting universal energy discovered in quantum mechanics that allows such a behavior.

This universal energy, what we will call the quantum web or universal hologram, both exists and expresses itself in different forms, frequencies, or vibrational levels (called quanta). It can thus be visible or invisible. Dr. Bohm calls the invisible vibrational frequencies "enfolded" or "implicate" energy and the visible forms or frequencies "unfolded" or "explicate" energy; in whatever form, whether visible or invisible, it is all essentially the same.

For example, we have the light spectrum (comprising both visible and invisible frequencies), electricity, radio waves, radiation, magnetism, fire, and so on. We also have solid matter: galaxies, solar systems, and planets. That includes our solar system, the Earth, and everything that exists on it, including rocks and trees and oceans and animals and people—us. In us we find both explicate, visible energy (our physical bodies) and implicate, invisible energy (consciousness) as expressed through thoughts, feelings, and emotions.

Again, regardless of how it is expressed, at its essence, energy is all still the same. All of it, all of creation, is made of this same stuff—energy. Energy is energy is energy, and thus everything that happens in this world we live in is simply the result of a connection, exchange, and interchange of quantum energy. Of course that must include us.

Throughout the science, from the earliest experiments involving the inanimate, basic particles of atoms (photons and electrons) to studies involving the most simple biological systems (organic molecules such as DNA and then single celled organisms) right through to experiments on the most complex (human beings), there is constant and consistent indication of organization and coordination, of communication and order through the connection and interconnection of quantum energy.

Life, then, is apparently a process of quantum energy exchange, energetic vibrational resonance and frequency. It is the music of quadrillions of atoms— fuzzy clouds of energy—buzzing about like so many sets of tiny hummingbird wings. Research overwhelmingly suggests that eventually biologists will have to recognize and accept this reality. In other words, like everything in the universe, biology *is* a quantum process.

Further, the experimental evidence indicates that this elemental universal energy field is not only everywhere and not only makes up everything, but it also apparently operates by intelligent design; one might think of it as pure consciousness, or, dare I use the phrase, pure spirit. After many years of experimentation and study of quantum science, the discipline he literally discovered, Max Planck stated, "All matter originates and exists only by virtue of a force.... We must assume [that] behind this force [is] the existence of a conscious and intelligent Mind. This Mind is the matrix of all matter."[2]

It is here that physics and metaphysics begin to overlap, the lines between science and spirit begin to blur, suggesting—actually demanding a reintegration of science, philosophy, and spirituality in order to understand fully how both our world and we work. One thing is certain: A universe consisting of one vast web or matrix of interconnected, seemingly intelligent energy turns the Newtonian-Darwinian model of independent, isolated, and separate systems and entities into an antiquated and apparently inaccurate relic.

This Mind, expressing through the universal energy or quantum web, as illustrated in countless experiments, responds or reacts to human thoughts, expectations, beliefs, and even emotions! After all, thoughts, expectations, beliefs, and emotions are really nothing more than another form or expression of the same thing: quantum energy. In other words, we are both a product of and contribute to the energy of our environment and everything in it. And we are essentially energetically connected to everything and everyone else that exists in our environment. This knowledge creates a new paradigm of what it means to be human. It makes us quantum beings!

ON BEING QUANTUM

What does it mean to be a quantum being in a quantum universe? It changes everything about the way we perceive our place in and interactions with the world around us. We can even think of ourselves, human beings, as holograms: Each of us comprises about 50 trillion cells, with each cell containing our entire complement of DNA; each cell in essence is a copy of the whole organism. Our cells form communities called organs and systems, which in turn form the larger entity we call the human organism.

Individual humans also behave—interacting with each person's environment—through connection and communication (although not always cooperative), both as an individual and with other humans, forming groups and communities: families, cities, states, countries, and so on, through the same feedback/feed-forward exchange of energy.

The symmetry and parallel of humanity with the model of a hologram and the idea of interconnectedness, a pattern that seemingly repeats throughout nature, is clearly evident. We can be likened to the flocks of birds or schools of fish, behaving in mass somewhat like a giant individual organism (See Figure 2 on the next page.) And in this regard, the notion of mass consciousness and memes gains further credibility. I find this idea fascinating.

The concept of a universe consisting of a distributed yet undivided holistic, holographic, and intelligent energy field, this model of connection and oneness between and among all matter and all beings also instantly evokes thoughts of the pervasively consistent worldview of the ancient cultures, the old ways. Somehow, these peoples intuitively knew and accepted then what modern science is proving now.

Perhaps it was through some innate, instinctive ability to perceive and tap into the energy of the quantum web that most of us in modern society have somehow forgotten. In other words, as we evolved and as our mass consciousness of collective ego tried to gain more and more mastery over the environment, we became increasingly more energetically imbalanced and thus continually more isolated from that energy field.

In time, we lost our ability to perceive and purposefully utilize this connection to the quantum web of energy we are made of, and in so doing also forgot our true nature and our place in the world. This may sound a little woo-woo—a little "out there," so to speak—but bear with me. I think you will see that it really is not so far-fetched an idea.

We know, for instance, that many of the other sentient creatures on the planet possess significantly greater sensory perception and abilities—keener sight, better smell, hearing, and more—than do we humans. In particular, they, the "lower" animals, often seem to sense and perceive impending events such as natural disasters well before they occur, and can thus seek shelter and safety. There are many stories of even domestic pets acting strangely just before the occurrence of a major environmental event such as an earthquake. We humans in modern society have apparently lost that innate perceptive ability.

Figure 2

The Human Hologram

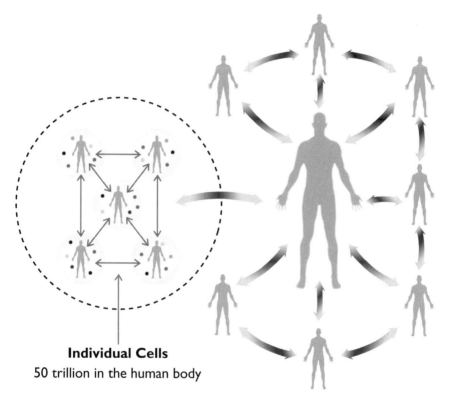

Individual Cells
50 trillion in the human body

Interconnectedness and the human hologram: Individual cells behave like tiny independent copies of the whole organism, connecting and interconnecting to one another and interacting with their environment through the exchange of energy. Together, these cells form the entity called the human being. The human being in turn connects to the energy of the universal hologram—the quantum web or matrix—and other humans in a similar fashion. Thus, in the order of nature, all energy and all beings are connected.

Yet the indigenous peoples who remain unexposed to modern society and thus more connected to the natural world—living the old ways—seemingly have not lost this sense. A telling example of this was seen in Indonesia and the Indian Archipelagos in 2005, when several aboriginal tribes moved to higher ground well before the devastating tsunami hit, and thus survived intact, whereas thousands of "civilized people" did not. They somehow knew it was coming.

Shortly after the event, there was a newspaper account of these people. A reporter named Roy wrote, "They can smell the wind. They can gauge the depth of the sea with the sound of their oars. They have a sixth sense which we don't possess."[3] With all due respect, Mr. Roy was incorrect. We *all* possess this extra sense—we're all the same species after all—but in modern, Western cultures, living under a crushing imbalance of energy, we have largely forgotten our ability to tap into it.

Stalking Wolf, also known as Grandfather, a Lipan Apache shaman who taught the old ways to world-famous outdoorsman, tracker, and spiritual teacher Tom Brown, Jr., often spoke of this sixth sense. He called it inner-vision, and described it as the power and voice of pure spirit: "The spirit that moves through all things."[4] He said that in the White world (Western Society) inner vision has grown vestigial and largely useless because we have forgotten the old ways of living in unity and balance with the natural world.

This opinion evokes the words of Gregg Braden's Wisdom Keeper, and the sentiments of Fools Crow quoted earlier. And what quantum science is now learning about the apparent energetic structure of the universe actually suggests an empirical, scientific basis for the existence of this energetic connection: a sixth sense, or inner-vision. And there is even more empirical (and very pragmatic) evidence for the existence of this energetic connection of inner-vision; most of us now and then still do experience at least hints of it and its power! On those occasions and in those moments in which we receive or feel what we call hunches, gut feelings, or intuitions about something, someone, or a situation, we are actually seeing, hearing, or feeling the energy of inner-vision giving us empowering guidance, but it is usually weak at best, and often ignored.

Another example of inner-vision at work is that discomforting feeling you may get from time to time that someone is watching you, and then when you look up, you see that someone is indeed focusing his or her attention upon you. These too are moments of inner-vision. For most of us in contemporary society, these moments of extraordinary awareness are rare. The rarity, intermittence, and weak interaction with inner-vision are the result of centuries of neglect.

REDEFINING AND RE-EVOLVING

Let us choose to accept the vast and growing empirical evidence indicating that the basis of the universe is a vast matrix of apparently intelligent energy—pure consciousness of Mind, as described by Max Planck—and let us also accept that we are an integral part of this matrix. Thus, in essence, we can also redefine ourselves and re-evolve in quantum terms. We are beings of pure consciousness (implicate energy) residing in a physical body (explicate energy).

This idea is important, as it also strongly affirms that we are not a body with a separate mind housed within our brain, as the conventional model defines us (remember Descartes?), but instead, a mind, a consciousness (that processes through the brain) within a body (the quantum model). London-based writer and philosopher Bryan Hubbard, a brilliant man with whom I have shared great conversation on this topic, likes to think of the human body as a "space-time suit" that consciousness inhabits in order to experience life in the physical realm—a metaphorical description I find both entertaining and rather apt.

It doesn't take much exploration to discover that this model is widely known. A great example can be found in the spiritual teachings of the Abraham-Hicks programs: More than 25 years ago, during meditation, Esther Hicks began to spontaneously channel a group of spiritual entities now known as "Abraham." What began as a very private experience for Esther and her husband, Jerry, has since evolved into an internationally renowned program of spiritual teaching.[5] These nonphysical spirit entities—Abraham—constantly remind readers and seminar audiences that humans are pure, positive, nonphysical (implicate) energy (consciousness or spirit) in a physical (explicate) manifestation (the body); vibrational beings in a vibrational universe having taken physical form. If we relearn to perceive and utilize the vibrational energy that moves through and connects all things everywhere, what power that would be!

THE HUMAN COMPUTER

There has to be an interface among the energy of spirit and consciousness (the mind), the energy of the physical (the body), and the quantum web. There must be a means through which to process the energy and experience of consciousness while in physical form. That means, of course, is our brain; what we might call the human computer. And, once again, according to the experimental evidence—much of it obtained through Stanford University neurophysiologist Karl Pribram's research—the human brain, as do all biological systems, seems to function according to quantum mechanics.

Pribram's theory, which he terms the holonomic brain theory, suggests that not only does the brain function through non-locality and interconnection—like the quantum web itself—but also that physical, objective reality is really only a perception. Pribram likens the process of brain function to the act of putting a lens on a blurry picture and focusing the lens to create clarity; it is our quantum observer.

If we remember that atoms, the building blocks of matter, are just energetic tendencies, indistinguishable fuzzy clouds of energy *until observed* (remember the blurry, buzzing hummingbird wings), it dovetails perfectly. Through our brain, we exchange energy with our environment (observe or participate) and that exchange creates our instantaneous perception of reality. Then, the environment responds and returns energy to us, which we then perceive, and on and on it goes.

What this means for all of us in essence is that what seems like objective reality *happening to us* is in actuality subjective reality *created by and through us*. In other words, we are back where we started, except now with science backing us up! Good or bad, happy or sad, healthy or sick, poor or abundant, we, all of us, create our reality through the exchange of energy with our environment. This is a critical construct upon which the models for Synthesis are predicated. Because we create our reality, if we don't like what we've created, we and only we have the power to change it!

Another way to express this is through a popular neuro-linguistic programming (NLP) paradigm. NLP is a science or technology that attempts to codify the how and why of human behavior and communication. In NLP, a key requirement for a successful therapeutic outcome is that one must transition from being at effect ("The world is happening to me; I am a victim of events and circumstances") to being at cause ("I am creating whatever I am experiencing, and I alone am responsible and have the power and resources to change it"). In Synthesis lie the models and tools for finding those resources and creating that change.

Through first understanding the basis of our creating the energetic reality of our existence, then learning how to reunite and reintegrate the corporal with the spiritual, we can change our perception and experiences in the world of explicate energy by learning to perceive and manipulate implicate energy. We thus become empowered to change a reality we don't like, first as individuals, and then, through the dissemination of new memes and social contagion via the human hologram, as empowered communities and societies, until finally, ultimately, as a species.

CHAPTER 2 SUMMARY
Takeaways

⇥ With the discovery of quantum mechanics, Western science is proving that it's been wrong. The universe is not a huge system of mechanistic, isolated systems, but instead composed of a vast, infinite field of energy—the quantum web or hologram—of which everything is made, and to which everything is connected and interconnected.

⇥ The energy of the quantum web, Source Energy, can be expressed in two primary ways: implicate enfolding (the invisible) and explicate unfolding (the visible).

⇥ Everything that exists is made of this Source Energy, and the true process of universal function is apparently one involving a constant exchange and interchange of this energy in both inanimate and living systems and entities. This includes us, humanity. We are quantum beings, a combination of implicate invisible energy (consciousness) and explicate, visible energy (our body).

⇥ Quantum theory and experimental evidence suggests that in order to create an explicate unfolding (something perceived as objective, visible reality), enfolded (invisible) implicate energy must be observed (acted upon in some way). We accomplish this "observation" through our mind and in the brain.

⊣ The process of consciousness interacting with the environment in effect acts as the observation needed to create the instant reality of matter; this is the basis and becomes our unique perception of physical reality.

⊣ Because each of us creates our own reality, only we as individuals have the ability to change a reality we do not like; we have powerful tools such as inner-vision, our predictive and protective sixth sense, to assist us in this process.

Action Items

⊣ Take some time to think of what it means to be a quantum being.

⊣ Review your past experiences to recall moments of inner vision—those moments of intuition, hunches, and gut feelings that served to guide you, and moments in which you did not pay attention and perhaps suffered for it.

⊣ Continue the process of further opening your mind to the possibilities of changing whatever you want to change.

⊣ Are you noticing a little more expectation, a little more anticipation for your outcome? If not, why not? Can you begin to shift your thinking to "believe in order to see" just a little?

⊣ Continue the daily breathing exercises, every single day.

Part II

Getting to Know You

Chapter 3:
Are You for Real?

One cannot help but be in awe when he contemplates the mysteries of eternity, of life, of the marvelous structure of reality.
—Albert Einstein

Quantum mechanics shows us that there is more to this world and our place in it than meets the eye—at least the eye of conventional Western science and philosophy. A quantum universe makes sense, adding increased order and logic to the mechanisms of the natural world and the essence and behavior of the most elemental bits of energy and matter that comprise everything in existence.

Still, it's one thing to read or hear about the science that is proving the quantum nature of the universe, as long as we keep it on the subatomic level; it is quite another for most people to wrap their brain around the concept that that they are in essence packets of pure energy expressed as consciousness housed in a physical body—their space-time suit—and that as quantum beings they create their own reality. That idea is not always quite so easy to swallow. This difficulty is especially prevalent if they are living a reality of pain and suffering—disconnection—a reality that is somehow more acceptable if they consider themselves the victims of their circumstances rather than the creators of them.

When I first introduce new clients to quantum reality, the initial response I often receive goes something like this:

"Are you for real? So, I'm a quantum being in a quantum universe, some-how—I still don't know how— creating my own reality, good or bad? So, this pain is *my* fault? It sure doesn't feel that way."

Or:

"Are you for real? You're saying *I did this to myself?* Ah, ha, ha, ha, I'm so sorry; I am quite sure it was my mother and father and my sixth-grade teacher, Ms. Gooblatz's fault—I mean, she laughed at me in front of the whole class, and then they told me it was no big deal! I was mortified, damaged for life!"

Or:

"Are you for real? You're telling me that my heartbreak wasn't Mr./Ms. Creep's fault, that slug who eloped with my former best friend a month after dumping me?"

And then, when I am gently adamant that, like it or not, their "it," what-ever "it" is, was indeed ultimately their doing, and that yes, I am for real and I mean what I say, I might hear something like:

"Okay, fine. Great. So now what? Just how is this knowledge supposed to help me live a better life? How can I use this quantum thing to get over Ms. Gooblatz, or Mr./Ms. Creep, or quit smoking, or lose weight, or get over my fears and phobias, or make more money, or have more confidence, or end my depression or anxiety, or manage my pain, or like myself more, or find a life partner, or eliminate whatever it is that's messing up my life, that's causing all this suffering? Gee, Doctor John, I thought I came here to get hypnotized and then *poof,* it all goes away."

"Sorry," I say. "That's just not for real. There's a little more to it."

This sort of reaction should not be surprising; it is simply a product of conventional Western thinking. There is a wonderful quote by an unknown author that sums it up nicely: "To err is human; to blame the next guy, even more so." Generally speaking, we are acculturated to find and blame something or someone else for the stuff in our lives that we find painful. We also tend to become very reactive in our thinking and behavior.

In other words, it usually feels as though life happens *to* us and then we react (feel and or behave) according to what happens. But in order to change your life, it is really important to realize and accept that what happens to you is ultimately the result of your energy, and your reactions usually create and perpetuate a repeating pattern and energy of disconnection.

When I first began to introduce Synthesis into my clinical practice and attempted to explain quantum reality to new clients, they repeatedly hit me with the old "I'll believe it when I see it" mindset. They wanted me to explain *how* it works. *How* do we create our own reality? What is the actual *process*?

This is a fair enough question, and not so easy to answer in words, particularly in the space of the relatively little time available in a clinical session, because it involves some rather abstract ideas. And we simply do not *feel* like little clouds of vibrating, resonating (or not) electromagnetic energy. We feel like a person named Bill or Sue, or Irving or Cathy, and we have this problem or issue that's happening to us. It hurts, and we just want to be rid of it.

And so I began to think about designing a simple, elegant model that would encapsulate all my years of reading and research, learning, self-reflection and self-growth; a model that would give all the Bills and Sues and Irvings and Cathys something they could see, dissect, and easily understand. The result, as displayed in Figure 3, is what I have come to call the Quantum Reality Equation.

THE QUANTUM REALITY EQUATION

The Quantum Reality Equation, the first of my four models of Synthesis, is a graphical "big picture" depiction of how we create our own reality in this miraculous process we call living. It is also designed to engage both sides of the brain: the analytical, quantitative left brain (the "Western" side) and the more reflective, abstract, creative right brain (the "ancient" or "quantum" side).

Figure 3

The Quantum Reality Equation

ENVIRONMENT (The Universe—The Quantum Web)

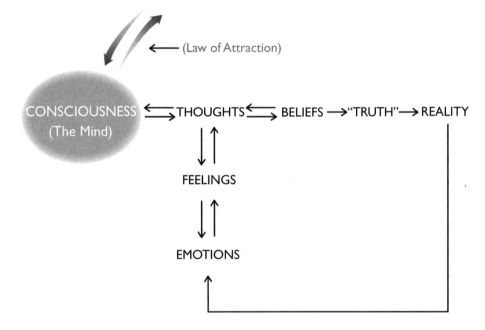

Understanding the mechanism and flow of quantum reality is best accomplished through a guided tour of this figure. Beginning on the left side, the circle represents the person—you or me or any one of the 7 billion members in this club we call humanity; the quantum energy of pure consciousness in our physical space-time suits. This process we call living is essentially a constant exchange and interchange of energies between our environment and us. We can think of the environment in any way we wish, but I like to include the whole universe because we are all part of it, and it represents limitless potential in terms of pure available creative energy.

This exchange and interchange of quantum energies, the product of consciousness interacting with its environment, creates internal energies that we call *thought*. The energies of thoughts in turn produce internal energies we call *feelings*, which of course interact with and are reflected by some of our most elemental energies—*emotions*. It is this internal feed-forward/feedback loop among thoughts, feelings, and emotions that produces what we perceive as contrast, and, as we discussed earlier, contrast is the very essence of the human existence.

Moving along the path, when and if the thoughts-feelings-emotions loops are repeated enough, they give rise to very powerful energies that we call *beliefs*. Our beliefs, once formed, become part of the bedrock of our behavior. Notice, too, that all the energy exchanges (signified by the arrows) up to the creation of beliefs are two-way, feed-forward/feedback exchanges. From the establishment of belief, though, we see a one-way path for the rest of the equation. The energy of our beliefs flows and leads to our *perception* of truth.

In *The Razor's Edge*, W. Somerset Maugham wrote, "The fact that a great many people believe something is no guarantee of its truth." It is essential to remember that what we believe or perceive as truth need not have any basis in actual fact. Regardless, our perceived truths in turn go on to frame and define our reality. Reality, once defined and perceived, feeds right back into the contrast loop of emotions, feelings, and thought. And on and on it goes, the constant interaction and exchange of energies between us and our environment producing the internal cycle that results in our reality; good or bad, happy or sad, pleasurable or painful, we create it.

THE ELEMENTS OF REALITY

Thoughts, Feelings, and Emotions

The energy loop involving thoughts, feelings, and emotions is what makes us unique among sentient creatures. It is also of course the product of our cognitive ability, the ability to reason and understand the concept of contrast. Although many of the other animals and creatures that we share the Earth with sometimes seem to understand and express human-like feelings and emotions, none of them approaches the human ability for cognition and abstract reasoning, and thus no other creature lives so completely in the realm of contrast.

To reiterate, contrast is the single-most important or defining element of our existence—to have or have not, be or be not, abundance or lack. So this loop in the reality equation becomes both a blessing and a curse. It allows us to feel the bliss and ecstasy of abundance, but only through knowing the comparative pain and despondence of lack and deficiency. Unfortunately, and as most of us know so well, so many, if not most, people in modern Western culture and society are dwelling on and manifesting a reality of lack. There is never enough—not enough money, not enough love, not enough peace, not enough health, and so on.

Beliefs and "Truth"

Returning to an earlier point, a "belief" can be defined as a thoughts-feelings-emotions loop that we repeat over and over again until it becomes automatic and ingrained. I first heard this description or definition of belief through the teachings of Jerry and Esther Hicks's "Abraham," and the more I considered it and thought about it, and the more I applied it to my own life, the more realistic and accurate it became for me. When you say, "I believe that..." you are simply repeating a thought that you've thought and felt many, many times, one that has become part of your very essence, and automatic.

The really interesting thing about beliefs is that they can be individual in nature or they can be the product of the thoughts transmitted by and through the mass consciousness of a society or culture. They then become the basis of memes, those cultural genes that we pass from one to another, which can so define our thinking and our existence.

Beliefs, then, are incredibly powerful energy. As we can see from the Quantum Reality Equation, once a belief is in place, it frames the perception of truth, and the perception of truth then determines one's reality, in a given moment, a particular time period, or even for a lifetime. To illustrate how powerful the energy of belief can be, we need only look at a phenomenon commonly known as the placebo effect.

The placebo effect is most often associated with medications and refers to the fact that often, individuals believing an inert placebo—usually a sugar pill—is in fact an active medication will actually derive and experience the medical benefits the medicine is suppose to bestow. In other words, the expectation created by the energy of belief creates the reality of the therapeutic effect.

The placebo effect has been clinically demonstrated thousands of times. In fact, it has been reported that many pharmaceutical companies have actually lobbied the FDA to eliminate the requirement for blind clinical trials for some new medications. The reason is that so often in these tests, the percentage of the control group test subjects—those given placebos or sugar pills—that derive the intended therapeutic medical benefits of the "drug" is virtually the same and sometimes even larger than that of the group actually taking the drug! The control group unwittingly believes in order to see, and then they do!

Another phenomenon that relates directly to the power of belief is observed in medical and psychological conditions and diseases. Often, once an individual is diagnosed with a medical or psychogenic condition, he or she incorporates the condition into his or her belief system. The person begins to identify him or herself by this condition or disconnection; for example, saying, "I am a cancer victim," "I am an insomniac," "I am depressed," or "I have ADHD," and thenceforth that belief defines the person's life, often creating a feeling of hopelessness regarding change or improvement.

Yet there are others who, even given a terminal diagnosis with no realistic hope for successful treatment, actually cure themselves through the power of thought, visualization, and faith or belief in their recovery. There is in fact a scientific discipline dedicated to the exploration of this phenomenon called psychoneuroimmunology.

Norman Cousins, former writer and editor-in-chief of the now-defunct *Saturday Review*, a national literary magazine, was one of the pioneers of this new science. Diagnosed with a terminal and untreatable illness, he cured himself through the power of belief in his recovery and the physiologically positive effects of the energy in humor. He later helped spearhead the initial development of the psychoneuroimmunology research program at UCLA. His story is fascinating, highly recommended, and, by the way, not at all unique. Many others have accomplished similarly miraculous cures. In a quantum model of reality, such an occurrence is much easier to accept as both plausible and logical. It is simply a matter of learning how to manipulate quantum energy purposefully.

In that regard, one vital point needs to be mentioned: As powerful as the energy of beliefs is, they are in essence nothing more than thoughts that have gained that power through repetition. And we can, any of us, control our thoughts! In fact, only you can control your thoughts. As I love to say, "It's your mind, you own it, and *only you* can control it." When I introduce the reality equation to a new client, and we discuss the subject of beliefs—how they are formed and the power they wield—I use a simple metaphor again and again. Although terribly cliché, it never fails to make the point both clearly and powerfully: Up until about 6,000 years ago, virtually every human being on the planet believed beyond a doubt that the Earth was flat. For the people of the time, this belief was a certainty, their "truth." And of course, even though it had no basis whatsoever in fact, this "truth" defined and created a quite limiting reality. Once Aristotle provided observational evidence to the contrary, this false and limiting belief began to erode (somewhat gradually in some quarters), with, I think it safe to state, significant and emancipating effects upon our reality.

Today we know beyond any doubt that the Earth is indeed a spheroid—not perfectly round, but close enough. We can see pictures of it from outer space, and it has been circumnavigated many hundreds of times. And so today, we are free of the limitations of these archaic beliefs, false truths, and that stifling reality. As such, we live a vastly different reality in terms of how we view our planet and what we can do on it than did our forebearers. With beliefs and truths based in fact, we live more freely and expansively than they could have even dreamed.

Individuals living under the burden of limiting beliefs such as the notion that they are "less than," unworthy, victims, or powerless to change their circumstances, are thinking Earth-flat thoughts, creating Earth-flat beliefs, and defining "truths" that have no basis in fact. These Earth-flat "truths" create an Earth-flat reality, limiting and often painful in some way.

The way to creating a reality of peace of mind and abundance is found through Earth-round beliefs—beliefs that define truths based on fact! It is actually, "We are all equally deserving of the abundance [in whatever form that takes] we desire, and we all have the capability to create that reality." Say it over and over: "The Earth is round, the Earth is round, the Earth is round! I am worthy, I do deserve—I do, I do, I do!" As we will see a little later, this thought can be used as a powerful tool and empowering mantra when practicing Synthesis.

THE LAW OF ATTRACTION

When you examine the Quantum Reality Equation in Figure 3, you no doubt notice that the arrows depicting the energetic interaction between our environment and us are labeled as the law of attraction. The law of attraction states simply this: That which is like unto itself is drawn. Many people have only recently become aware of its existence, and largely through the significant media exposure of books and films such as *The Secret*. The law of attraction is thus considered by many to be something very New Age and rather avant-garde.

In truth, the law of attraction has been recognized as a physical and energetic law, and has been taught throughout human history. For example, it is mentioned in the Bible in one way or another more than 200 times, in both the Old and New Testaments. For example, Proverbs 23:7 states, "As a man thinketh, so he is"; Galatians 6:7 states, "Do not be deceived, God cannot be mocked, a man reaps what he sows."

It is through this fundamental law of energy exchange and interaction that we live, and in living generate our reality equations. Think about this salient fact: The natural flow of universal energy is one of attraction. For example, gravity—a clearly universal energy—does not repel objects; it attracts them! And the same goes for you and me. What we energetically project into our environment—the universe—through the focus of our attention, thoughts, and actions *must* be returned in kind; good or bad, it does not matter.

That statement, "good or bad, it does not matter," is of key importance. Remember, at least on Earth, and as far as we can tell, only we humans live completely in the grip of contrast—good or bad, lack or abundance, and so on. In nature, energy is energy is energy. How it is expressed is irrelevant. Newton's third law of motion states that for every action there is an equal and opposite reaction. "Opposite" does not necessarily imply opposite energy, but just an equal amount of energy flowing in the opposite direction.

You might think of yourself as an energy transmitter, and your environment—the universal quantum web of energy—as a giant receiver, amplifier, and reflective transmitter. So, if you focus on and transmit the energy of lack, you attract more lack. If you learn to focus on and transmit the energy of wellbeing and abundance (whatever that means to you), you must attract wellbeing and abundance. It is law. Another way I like to think about this is to remember the old saw, "Birds of a feather flock together." You don't see crows hanging out with pigeons, or sparrows hanging out with hawks. Like attracts like, and that includes positive and negative attitudes, beliefs, behaviors, values, and people.

Going back to some of the early experiments in quantum physics that I described in the last chapter, when scientists were trying to observe the different states (particle or wave) of energetic entities such as photons or electrons, they repeatedly and uncannily observed the energy in the state they *expected* to see. In other words, their projected energy in the form of hopes and expectations for the outcome of a given experiment attracted like energy back, and, in turn, produced the results they focused on.

This was and is one of those bothersome issues for scientists dealing with quantum mechanics, as the phenomenon happened and happens over and over again. Of course, the law of attraction explains these results quite nicely. For me, a classically trained, scientific, and very pragmatic individual, I love the fact that this law is observed and verified under strict scientific conditions, which clearly elevates it beyond the world of esoteric woo-woo!

Because we literally create our own reality, it seems obvious that all we need do is learn to harness this law of attraction and attract everything we wish to have. Sounds simple enough, doesn't it? And in essence, it is! "Then why," as so many of my clients will immediately ask, "does it not seem even remotely possible? I swear that all this pain, suffering, and lack I'm feeling feels like it's *happening to* me, not *created by* me. I clearly need help here."

The truth is that most of us do need a little help in order to accomplish something that is simplicity itself—creating a new reality through manipulating the Quantum Reality Equation and the law of attraction. In order to understand why this is so, we must peek under the hood and take a closer look at the circle in the equation: the human being. Pure consciousness, spirit, mind; the creator and processor of the experience of life, housed in a physical body—its space-time suit.

We must first understand how the mind develops and how it functions; *how* we become who and what we are, and *why* we think and behave the way we do as individuals. Then, we can also consider the whole being, such as how the human energy system is organized and functions. In so doing, we will find the answers to the apparent irony of feeling as if we're at the mercy of circumstance (at effect) while actually being the creator (at cause) of whatever our lives become.

All this should be quite helpful to you in really getting to know *you*, and I will be introducing more models to help it all make simple and pragmatic sense. First, though, I'd like to share my earliest real experience with successfully manipulating the law of attraction and the Quantum Reality Equation. It happened many years ago, and at the time, I had no idea what I was doing. I now do, and I delight in sharing this experience, both with my clients and with you.

THE NEW PHILOSOPHY

During my middle school, high school, and college years, I had a summer job working on the grounds maintenance crew at a local public golf course owned by my uncle. The crew was traditionally composed of area kids, many of whom would start working at the course after about the seventh or eighth grade, doing odd gofer-like jobs or washing golf carts; whatever chores needed doing.

With each new summer, as we grew older, we would move up the ranks until we were actually taking care of the golf course, cutting, watering, and fertilizing the grass, along with a myriad of other projects. One summer I got to design and build a bridge across one of the course's several water hazards. Working on the crew was an awesome summer job. We got to work outside, made decent money, and once we were actually on the crew we got to operate real equipment such as mowers, sprayers, tractors, and even an old dump truck—all a thrill for most teenagers (at least it was for us).

As I mentioned, the kids who were lucky enough to be hired tended to come back every summer, and as the years went by, we grew up together and became good friends. We worked together and, especially after we got our driver's licenses with the enormous independence that comes with that marvelous teenage rite of passage, we hung around together after work, too. We were together day and night all summer long. We were a tribe, a community.

I believe it was toward the end of final exams during my sophomore year in college that I experienced what I felt was an epiphany in my thinking and created what I then simply called "The New Philosophy." The New Philosophy wasn't really so earth-shattering in structure and content; it simply involved a conscious choice to look at the half-full glass in situations and occurrences rather than the half-empty glass, which had been my normal bent. In other words, I decided to purposely look for and find the positive aspects of everything that I experienced, no matter what. It became almost like a game to me.

I don't recall exactly what triggered the choice to do this consciously and consistently. It may have been osmosis from my Great Aunt Irene, who actively subscribed to and practiced the power of positive thinking as taught by the Science of Mind movement created by Ernest Holmes. To this day, I can say without hesitation that I have never known a more positive person than Aunt Irene, or "Aunt I" as we called her, and with whom as a youngster I spent a good part of every summer in the idyllic setting of her small farm in rural New Hampshire.

So, here it was, the summer of 1972, and I couldn't wait to get home to Connecticut and see my crew buddies to share what I had discovered. The night before we were to begin our summer jobs, we got together for some celebratory libations at a favorite watering hole called Harry's Bar and Grill. It was over a couple of pitchers of cold, frosty brews that I explained the New Philosophy to my cohorts and convinced each of them—there were about five or six of us in the core group—to sign up for the whole summer. The agreement I sought from them was that no matter what happened, we would all, together, look for the positive, look to learn, and then stay the positive course as we moved on.

Thinking back it was just a bit ironic that this occurred at Harry's, for Harry himself was one of the dourest, sourest, and most negative people I had or have ever encountered. I never once saw the poor man smile! He also didn't like young people much, and would glare as he poured our pitchers and took our money. As I think back to the grim atmosphere he created in his tavern, I wonder now why we even went there. Anyway, everyone signed up. We had a pact, and the next morning we reported for our first day of work at the golf course.

It was a complete rainout. It poured! So we sat in the maintenance building, swapping school stories, and celebrating the positive that we had found in the moment: the fact that, although we were not making any money, we had the chance to catch up and begin planning our summer exploits. Throughout that summer, we stuck to the pact, and I can tell you that it was the most euphoric three months of my young life. Nothing bothered us, nothing seemed to phase us, and we had more fun together, met more women, and made more money than ever. I looked forward to every single day, even the days when I had drudge duty such as digging drainage ditches. The group and I radiated optimism, virtually all the time, and we busted one another for the inevitable slips that occurred. I now realize that what we did was surround ourselves with pure, positive expectations for ourselves as individuals and as a group, a community, and the law of attraction reciprocated. It was truly an amazing and empowering experience.

Unfortunately, when we all parted for school that September, I allowed myself to forget the practice, and fell right back into my normal glass-half-empty attitude and patterns. It happened to all my mates too. And by the time we got back together for our last summer together, the one before senior year, graduation, and entering the "real world," The New Philosophy was left languishing in the somewhat fetid realm of good but forgotten intentions. Our last summer together was a shadow of the former one.

The feeling and attitude of The New Philosophy resurfaced for me from time to time, but only for relatively brief periods. The summer of The New Philosophy was just a preview; it would take more than 20 additional years to discover the real essence of it and make it a permanent way of living as I have learned to do, and as I teach my clients to do.

I had much to learn. I had to learn how and why my mind worked the way it did—usually dwelling on the half-empty—and I had to learn what was required to change that mechanism into one that was instead about celebrating the half-full—no, wait; why not try creating and celebrating the glass being completely full? "Is that possible?" many ask. My answer: "Yes indeed! And well worth it." It begins with understanding and embracing a simple, universal law combined with one central idea: "That which is like unto itself is drawn," and, "It's all in your mind."

CHAPTER 3 SUMMARY
Takeaways

⇾ The Quantum Reality Equation is designed to help you understand the actual process through which you create your reality via the exchange and interchange of energy between you and your environment, and also within you.

⇾ Thoughts, feelings, and emotions are the internal energies that express our processing of contrast, the central essence of the human experience.

⇾ Beliefs are a very powerful expression of thoughts repeated until they become automatic, and then the definers of our perception of truth.

⇾ The perception of truth, factual or not, frames the basis of our reality.

⇾ The law of attraction is a universal law concerning the flow of energy. The energy you project or transmit into the quantum web is received, amplified, and reflected back at you. This includes your thoughts, attitudes, expectations, beliefs, and the resulting behavioral choices you make every day, 24/7.

Action Items

⇾ Review the metaphor of believing in a flat Earth versus round Earth. Which reality would you rather live?

⇾ Your beliefs are reflective of your core values. Think about your beliefs; how many of them are based in actual fact? Are you living any Earth-flat beliefs and therefore "false truths" about yourself and your life?

⇾ You can see through the Quantum Reality Equation that as you project energy, you receive like energy back via the law of attraction.

Learning how to manipulate the law of attraction will be very important for your process in Synthesis; continue focusing on increasing your expectations for change

⇥ Review the story of The New Philosophy. Notice how many of the concepts we've discussed were evident that summer: the law of attraction, the power of a cooperative community (a tribe), and our creating and passing thought patterns or memes that in turn affected our group's mass consciousness and behavior, all of which then had a direct effect on our reality.

⇥ Continue the daily breathing exercise; do it every day, at least once a day.

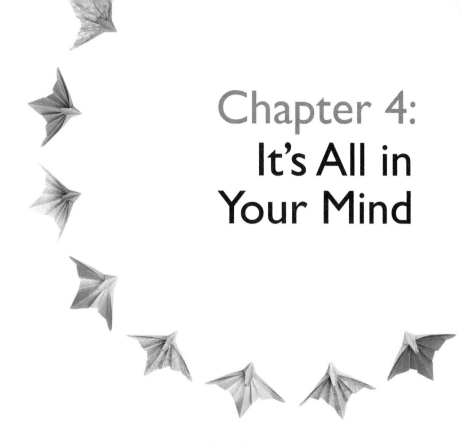

Chapter 4:
It's All in Your Mind

The mind is everything. What you think you become.
—Gautama Buddha

Stacy, an attractive 34-year-old marketing professional, sat in the guest chair facing my desk. Her facial expression and body language reflected a mix of energy and emotion typical of most new clients at their first session; there is a palpable uncertainty and nervousness combined with an almost prayerful desire for a successful outcome. Stacy had come in for help in overcoming what she had described on the telephone as nearly constant worry and low-grade anxiety, lack of confidence, and very low self-esteem.

I began the session by asking her the same basic questions I ask of every new client. "Why are you here? Or better, what will be different about you when we're finished working together?"

She replied, "I'm always second-guessing myself, worrying about what people think of me, and I'm tired of feeling like I always come last; even with myself, I come last."

I took a note, and then asked, "When did you begin treating yourself so unkindly?"

She hesitated for few seconds as the question registered, then replied, "I don't know; I can't remember a specific time."

I jotted down another note. "Okay, how did you learn to be so constantly worried and anxious?"

She quickly replied, "I don't really know that either; I just feel this feeling of being overwhelmed all the time. I worry about everything. *What if this happens, or what if that happens?* And then, not only do I worry, I always *expect* the worst."

I asked, "Do you notice the worst happening?"

"Not always, but yeah, a lot of times it seems that way."

Finally, I asked, "Is there anything else?"

She said, "It's just this feeling that I have. I feel so alone. No one seems to care about what I want, but I'm always driving myself crazy and worrying about pleasing others, about how they will feel, or what they want."

"How long have you felt like this?" I asked.

"Oh my God, I don't know. It seems like forever; as long as I can remember." Tears began to flow. "And I hate it. I hate the way I feel!"

Stacy's despair and not knowing the reason for coming to behave and feel the way she did about herself is a very common pattern. In fact, I find this to be the case with many, if not most new clients. Regardless of their issue, they come in with that same sort of "broken" feeling, and without conscious knowledge as to how or why they got that way. Worse, they have often tried to break out of their dysfunctional feelings and behaviors with absolutely no success. I become their last resort.

This is typical of the human condition. Our behavioral and emotional habits and patterns become so ingrained, so part of the essence of our lives, so automatic, that we cannot remember feeling or acting any differently. It hurts, and we don't like it; logically we know it's not healthy, that we are getting in our own way, but that's the way it is. We also often don't have a clue as to how to change it. If we've tried, what we've tried hasn't worked.

To actually witness the anguish and despair Stacy expressed in our first conversation would make it difficult to believe that within just a few short weeks she left my office after her fifth and last session wearing a radiant smile, glowing with an air of ease, confidence, and well-being. Two months later, she called to tell me she had met and was seeing "a great guy," and six months after that, she was engaged.

It has now been two years since we worked together. Stacy recently sent word that she got a promotion to a senior management position in her company and is expecting her first child—quite a turn-around from where she was when she first came to see me. The very good news is that Stacy's success is not the exception, but rather the rule with my clients. But just how did she do it? How did she transcend herself and her disconnection—anxious, worrisome, self-deprecating, and isolated—and become a dynamo of optimism, happiness, achievement, and unbridled potential? It was all in her mind.

Nothing in your experience can happen without the participation—the perception, processing, and responses—of your mind. There is a well-worn platitude we constantly hear and read in the world of personal growth and self-help: *Change your mind, change your life*. Although that statement is completely hackneyed and absolutely cliché, it is also quite true. The mind is the central processor of everything we associate with the experience we call living. Thus, in order to change the way you experience and process your life, your reality equation, you must change the operation of the processor, the mind. "But how do I do that?" you might ask. "I've tried and tried and nothing has ever worked."

I'm going to show you how, but as always, we must continue the process of setting context. Understanding how your mind developed and how it works— just like understanding your car engine's systems, if you remember that metaphor from the Introduction—makes using the tools and effecting the repair and healing much easier and more powerful.

M4: THE MCGRAIL METAPHORICAL MIND MODEL

Almost as many theories and models have been postulated about the structure and function of the human mind and the dynamics of human behavior as there are psychologists, behavioral theorists, neurophysiologists, biochemists, and so on. And, truly, I suppose a case can be made for the veracity of many of them.

From a pragmatic, therapeutic perspective, however, I believe the best model is one that can help virtually anyone understand the dynamics of the mind, and thus themselves and their behaviors, both logically and quickly. It should explain how and why we develop our negative emotional and behavioral patterns, how and why we become stuck in them, and therein suggest what must be done to get unstuck. To accomplish that task, I developed the McGrail Metaphorical Mind Model, or M4.

M4 is based upon a mind theory first postulated by Dr. John Kappas, founder of the Hypnosis Motivation Institute in Los Angeles, and taught to all students of the college for use in their practice. Yet M4 has been extensively modified from the Kappas model to accommodate the science of quantum reality and other widely accepted theories of behavioral development, including my own, all making it much easier to use the tools of Synthesis to create rapid and permanent change and personal growth.

Reflective of its title, and as you will see, M4 is metaphorical; the complexities of the biochemistry, neurobiology, and neurophysiology of the mind are not really important for our purposes. What *is* important is what we see, feel, and observe. The M4 model builds sequentially, step by step, from birth to adulthood, and from the deepest subconscious to the cognitive conscious. There are diagrams included along the way to help illustrate the process and the results.

I love showing M4 to new clients such as Stacy because it always produces a wonderful moment of discovery: "Aha, I get it! Now I at least understand how and why I am what I am, how and why I'm feeling and behaving the way I am, how and why I've been stuck, and how and why I haven't been able to get unstuck." This "aha" moment helps lift the cloud of despair and hopelessness, helps kindle expectation, and thus opens the portals to creating change and transformation.

We can think of the human mind as composed of two primary parts or components: the conscious and the unconscious or subconscious. The subconscious component consists of three subdivisions: the animal or primal mind, the lower subconscious (or super-conscious), and the upper subconscious, each with its own functionality (See Figure 4).

Notice, as shown in Figure 4, that the vast majority (about 88 to 90 percent) of the "real estate" or mass of the mind is taken up by the subconscious component. The mind functions through the process of the conscious and subconscious interacting with one another, producing the phenomenon we call consciousness. It is consciousness, the essence of all life—pure quantum energy—interacting with its environment that creates the experience we call living.

Figure 4

THE MCGRAIL METAPHORICAL MIND MODEL—M4
Structural Overview

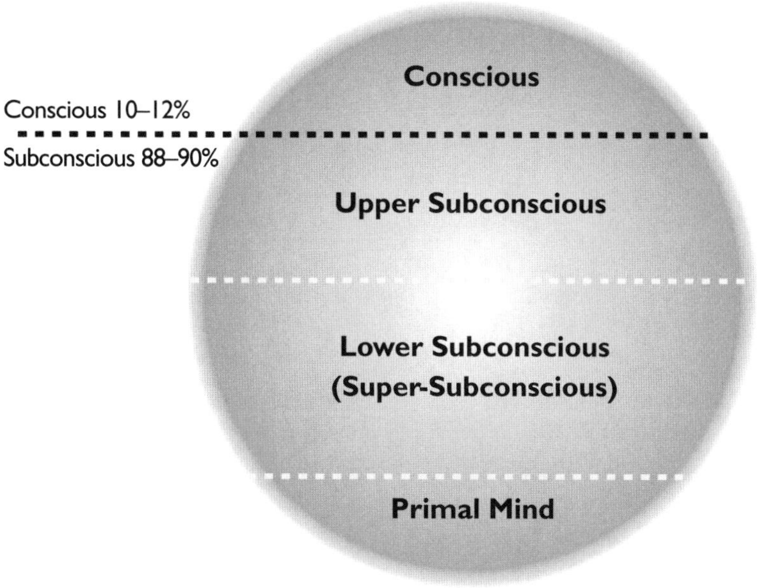

Conscious

Conscious 10–12%

- -

Subconscious 88–90%

Upper Subconscious

**Lower Subconscious
(Super-Subconscious)**

Primal Mind

The Mind at Birth

When we are born, the "higher" levels of the mind—the upper subconscious and the conscious—are basically empty. An apt analogy is to liken the upper subconscious and the conscious mind to a brand-new and very powerful computer with an empty hard drive and central processor: lots of capacity and potential computing power, but no data in the operating system. Of course, you cannot remember this part of your life, but if you ever have the opportunity to watch a newborn, it's easy to see that there really isn't much going on. There is life, consciousness, but at birth, only the primal mind and the lower subconscious or super-conscious have formed and are actually functioning.

The most primitive part of the subconscious component of the mind—the primal mind—is pictured at the bottom of the M4 diagram (see Figure 5).

Figure 5

M4: The Mind at Birth
THE PRIMAL MIND

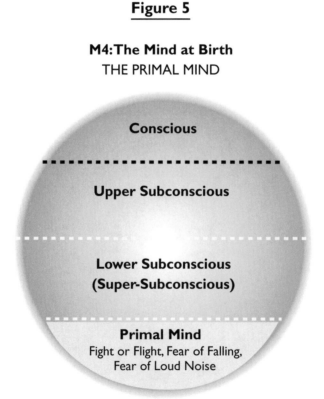

Conscious

Upper Subconscious

Lower Subconscious
(Super-Subconscious)

Primal Mind
Fight or Flight, Fear of Falling,
Fear of Loud Noise

The primal mind has one vitally important job, and that is to assure our basic survival—maintain and regulate the life force of the organism. It is the control center for autonomic or automatic physiological functionality: respiration, circulation, digestion, metabolism, and so on. It is also the center for the survival instinct, known as the fight or flight response. Fight or flight is triggered by a perceived threat from the environment; it is the emotional and physiological response that we call stress and fear. Notice, however, that at birth a human baby can feel and express only two fears: the fear of falling and the fear of loud noise (refer to Figure 5). Thus, any and all other fears we experience and feel later in life, whether they are real and rational (the results of actual threats) or completely irrational (what we call phobias) are learned.

Moving up, the next subdivision—the lower subconscious or super-conscious (see Figure 6) is the seat of very elemental, powerful, and integrally related energies: unconditional love, self-esteem, and spirit—the energy of pure consciousness, our soul.

Figure 6

M4: The Mind at Birth
THE LOWER SUBCONSCIOUS

Conscious

Upper Subconscious

Lower Subconscious
(Super-Subconscious)
Unconditional Love, Self-Esteem, Spirit,
Source Energy, Inner Vision

Primal Mind
Fight or Flight, Fear of Falling,
Fear of Loud Noise

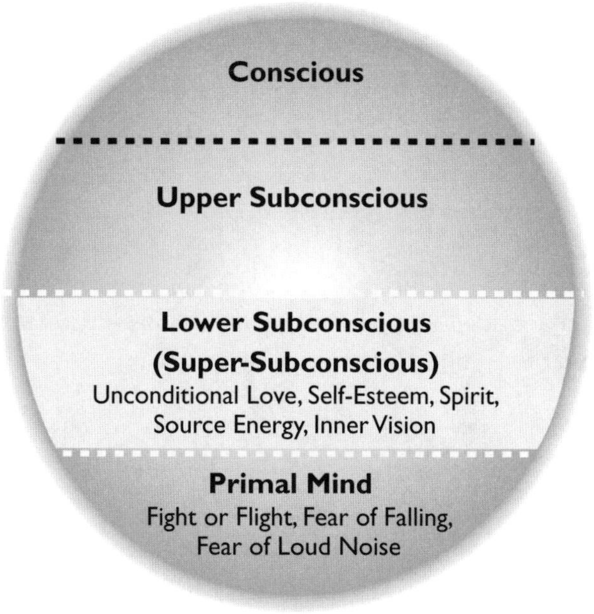

Unconditional love is often referred to as the only true or pure emotion we can feel. Because at birth we have as yet no ego, there are also no ego-related conditions attached to our giving and receiving love. We all come into this life chock full of pure, unconditional love, both for ourselves and for anyone who gives it to us. We are all born fully and rightfully in love with ourselves.

When we are very little, we also know that we are perfect little beings, and thus full of vastly abundant and perfectly formed self-esteem, an adjunct of our unconditional love. At birth and early in life no one has yet begun to tell us that we are "less than" or "not enough."

Also in those early days, we have yet to learn to care about what anyone else thinks of us, and we have no concept of failure, which is a good thing. For instance, when we learn to walk we "fail" (fall on our butts) hundreds of times before we can actually stand on our wobbly little legs and move under our own power. And even after we get it, we still have a long way to go before it's easy to do. Can you imagine trying to learn to walk with an adult concept of failure? After a few dozen failures you'd likely just sit there and lament, "I'm a failure; I'm done with this!" And that might be that; you'd never walk.

As for spirit, again it is the energy of our essence, our soul. It is our connection to the energy of Source, the energy of all creation; we can call it our connection to our higher power, or to God, or that part of God that lives within us. Spirit is also the basis of inner vision; that *very* powerful, predictive, and protective energy briefly described earlier. We will discuss how to tap into and use the power and potential of inner vision in great detail a little later on.

It is also possible that the lower subconscious/super-conscious also contains the energy of memories from our soul's or spirit's past lives, but at birth the upper subconscious and conscious components, whose functionality would be required to retrieve and process these memories, have not yet developed; therefore, we are incapable of doing so. Later in life, of course, that may well be possible, and tapping into past-life memories can and may be a powerful vehicle for healing for some individuals.

Development of the Mind: Imprinting

The first major period of the mind's development is called imprinting, and it occurs largely between birth and about 8 years of age. An awful lot happens during imprinting, particularly in terms of developing the conscious and the upper subconscious. It is during imprinting that we basically become us, the person. This is also the one time in life when we are completely at the mercy of the inputs from our environment; initially these inputs are largely acquired through the aegis of our parents or primary caregivers.

In some philosophical quarters, there is a prevailing notion that we—our soul or spiritual being—pre-choose the circumstances of each of our lives (our parents and the environment in which we will develop) in order to ensure we learn whatever lessons that we, along with our spiritual teachers, have decided we need in order to further our spiritual evolution. True or otherwise, it is in the imprinting stage that the upper subconscious, the hard-drive of the mind, is programmed, and it is the upper subconscious that largely defines us as a person.

This fact is vitally important: The upper subconscious is very much a data-recording, storage, and playback machine; it is incapable of distinguishing between reality and illusion, true or false, good or bad. Further, and this is also really important, it only knows present time and it never matures past the age of about 3. As such, like any little child, it is completely innocent, receptive, and suggestible; it will basically believe whatever it is told.

The upper subconscious also becomes what we might call the seat of personal identity, or the ego. And it is worth repeating that most of the personal attributes that we express as adults are imprinted or programmed during these critical, formative years, and are stored here. Yes, by the time we reach the ripe old age of 8, our internal database is pretty much formed in terms of our personality, attitudes, core values, and core beliefs; almost all the characteristics of the adult we are to become! This is not to say that there is no more development later on, but the bulk of our subconscious programming happens very early in life.

The Imprinting Process

The upper subconscious is essentially imprinted or programmed through a learning process called association and identification. As we begin to experience life, we use our senses to process the inputs/experiences/suggestions we receive. These inputs/experiences/suggestions pass through the conscious mind into the upper subconscious, where it records them (associates and identifies them) as basically either positive or negative. As you may know, computers utilize a very simple system to operate called "base two": on or off, yes or no. Positive or negative is the essential human computer language, our "base two," so to speak, the essence of our primordial meme—contrast.

During imprinting, if a given input/experience/suggestion is a minor, one-time event, or if it's transient, occurring only very occasionally, the upper subconscious will generally not record a permanent record of it. If, on the other hand, a given input/experience/suggestion receives appropriate reinforcement through repetition or through significance—for example, if it is traumatic enough—the association and identification become ingrained and "permanent."

Dr. Kappas called these ingrained, recorded programs and patterns of feelings, emotions, and behavior, "knowns." Once a known is created, its given environmental input/experience/suggestion automatically results in a corresponding output: a thought, feeling, emotion, or behavior. We might also think of them as "apps" or "autos" that play on cue, or like an electrical circuit; flip the switch (provide an input) and the light turns on (we respond with a feeling/attitude/ behavior) every time. Knowns are signified in Figure 7 by the plus and minus signs.

Knowns form the basis of your personality, attitudes, values, learned self-image, all learned fears, and all the emotions associated with the conditionally based ego. Basically, the upper subconscious becomes the veritable engine of behavior, and once established, the database of knowns triggers your default emotional and behavioral responses to life's experiences.

Knowns also form the basis of your belief system about yourself and your world. It is worth repeating that your beliefs frame your perception of truth, which creates your sense of reality. For example, if as a little child you were repeatedly told, "Sweetheart, always remember that you can do anything you set your mind to. You are smart and talented and you deserve and can always have the very best in life," this suggestion would become a "known" and the basis of a belief and perception of truth about yourself that would certainly have an effect on your reality.

If, on the other hand, you repeatedly heard, "Why can't you be more like your brother? He was always the best at everything he did, and just look at what a success he's become; as lazy as you are, you'll never get very far," this suggestion would also become a "known" and the basis of a belief and perception of truth about yourself that would also have a significant effect upon your reality. And it would likely be a rather painful and limiting one at that.

Figure 7

M4: Imprinting
DEVELOPMENT OF THE UPPER SUBCONSCIOUS PROGRAMS
("KNOWNS")

Environmental Inputs

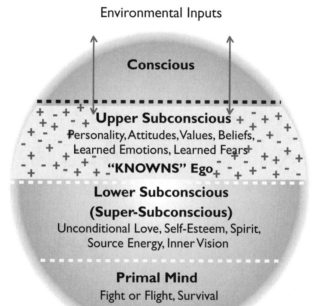

As we grow and develop, the sphere of exposure, the spectrum or range of inputs that create and reinforce our subconscious programming and the formation of knowns naturally expands. We begin life under the exclusive domain of parental (or our primary caregivers') contact and influence, and then, as our world expands, we are exposed to inputs from our siblings, friends, teachers, the media, and so on, until eventually we are thoroughly exposed to the prevailing attitudes, conditions, and cultural mores and memes of society at large—what we call mass consciousness.

This is how you come to be and reflect an amalgam, how part of *you* is reflective of *us*. It is how part of you almost surely reflects some or all of the seven deadly memes: obsession with lack, incessant desire for control and comfort, isolation, the Great Separation, empiricism, conditional love, and falsely (externally) derived self-esteem, basing our sense of worth on the opinions of others.

One of the major results of the exposure to and imprinting of the seven deadly memes is that a "barrier" (as depicted by the dark band in Figure 8) develops between the two parts of the subconscious, and we become blocked off from the immensely powerful energy and essence of our lower subconscious.

Figure 8

M4: Socialization
DISCONNECTING FROM THE SUPERCONSCIOUS

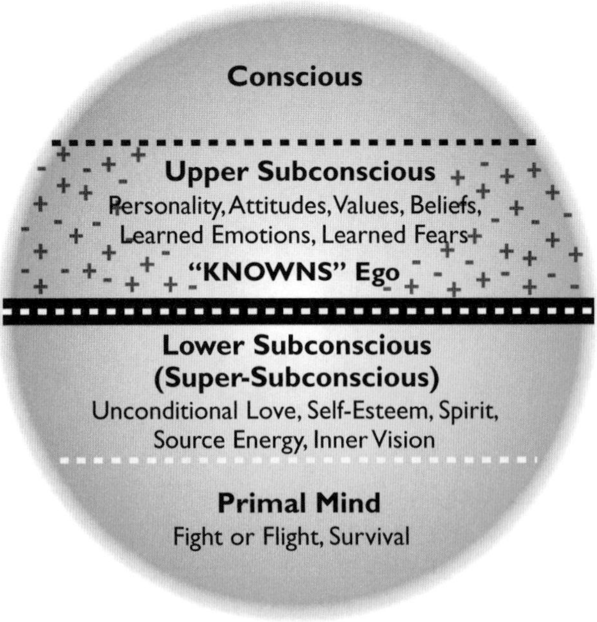

Conscious

Upper Subconscious
Personality, Attitudes, Values, Beliefs,
Learned Emotions, Learned Fears
"KNOWNS" Ego

**Lower Subconscious
(Super-Subconscious)**
Unconditional Love, Self-Esteem, Spirit,
Source Energy, Inner Vision

Primal Mind
Fight or Flight, Survival

Losing our connection to the superconscious energy of unconditional love, self-esteem, and spirit creates knowns that are self-disparaging rather than self-empowering, and this is a major cause of the pinging, chugging, and wheezing—disconnection— affecting most behavioral engines today. We learn to receive and give love conditionally. We learn to doubt ourselves and to rely on others for validation and our sense of value—others whose values, opinions, and expectations (even those of our parents) are often quite different from ours and also quite negative—resulting in fear, anger, stress, anxiety, and a pervasive feeling of lack and isolation, and thus also perpetuating the seven deadly memes.

In short, the powerful energies of our lower subconscious or super-conscious are essentially lost to us like a treasure that went down with a Spanish Galleon in a storm off the Florida Keys. Like the treasure, they are still there, of course, but they get buried under the sands and silt of neglect that through tides and time get thicker and thicker until we can no longer connect to them. Like Stacy, we learn to believe that we are "less than," "not enough," or "unworthy."

Development of the Conscious Mind

The principal development of the conscious mind also occurs during imprinting, between birth and about 5 years of age. As you can see in Figure 9, the conscious mind is the seat of logic and reasoning. Free will (willpower) and our voice are also part of conscious functionality. It is indeed these conscious energies that make us unique among species; they provided the evolutionary edge that allowed us to take over the planet.

It is also important to remember that as powerful as our cognitive functions are, the conscious only comprises about 10 to 12 percent of the total mass or power of the average mind. In other words, the subconscious is a much more powerful contributor to our normal day-to-day behaviors, attitudes, and feelings. The knowns of the upper subconscious mostly run the show, and mostly automatically.

Figure 9

M4: Imprinting
DEVELOPMENT OF THE CONSCIOUS MIND

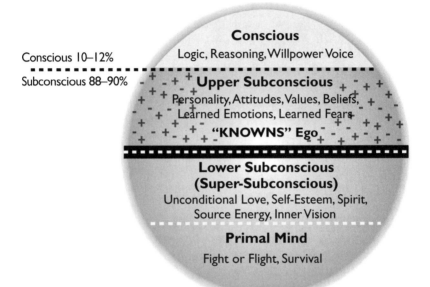

As a former military and airline pilot, and similar to many others, including Dr. Bruce Lipton in *The Biology of Belief,* I like to compare the conscious and subconscious to a pilot and autopilot. The conscious mind—the pilot—is the creative, active part of consciousness. It can conjure thoughts on purpose and create intention. The subconscious—the autopilot—is strictly habitual, reflective, and reactive in nature. When stimulated by an environmental trigger (input/experience/suggestion) it automatically responds with or plays the recordings—knowns—positive or negative, that it was programmed with during imprinting.

Dr. Lipton also notes another significant difference between the two parts of the mind: The conscious mind operates at a much slower speed than the subconscious. He states that the subconscious processes some 20,000,000 environmental stimuli per second compared to a mere 40 for the conscious.

Another interesting note in this regard is that the conscious mind not only operates slower, but it is also evolutionarily designed to focus efficiently on only one task or event at a time. Thus, the current trend that so celebrates and promotes multitasking in modern Western culture is really quite inefficient from a biological or neuro-physiological perspective. Just imagine what might have happened to our forbearers if, while out hunting for food, they had been as into multi-tasking as many of us are today. Chances are they would have *become* food instead of procuring it! I was recently witness to an excellent example of this idea, although the consequences in this particular instance were fortunately less dire.

While driving home from the clinic one evening, I happened to glance over at the car next to me. It caught my attention because it was traveling rather more slowly than the stream of traffic. Alone in the car was a young woman who was animatedly talking on her cell phone, drinking a soda, smoking a cigarette, and somehow—I don't know how, maybe with her knees because both hands were already occupied—driving her car, all at the same time!

Up ahead, the traffic light turned red and everyone slowed down...that is, almost everyone. Sure enough, this multitasker crunched right into the car ahead of her. Bang! Fortunately, she was already moving slowly so not much more than her ego was damaged, yet in the days of hunting and gathering, I'm quite sure she would have become food.

Multitasking is largely inefficient and potentially unsafe, and at the very least, a stress producer. Don't we have enough of that in our lives already? Whenever I work with clients who have academic issues, or testing issues, or concentration issues, part of the program is always to re-teach them how to be present and consciously focused on one and only one task or thought at a time. The results are often nothing short of amazing.

Development of the Mind, Phase 2: Modeling

Between the ages of about 8 and 14 we enter the second phase of mind development, known as modeling. Our subconscious knowns—values, habits, beliefs, and the resulting behaviors—become progressively more ingrained and more automatic; we begin to model and perfect them. Also, a mental "filter" develops between the conscious and subconscious. We'll call this the critical filter, depicted by the light gray band in Figure 10 on the next page.

Figure 10

M4: Imprinting
DEVELOPMENT OF THE CRITICAL FILTER

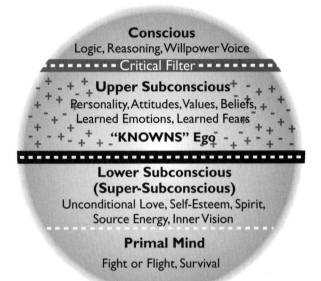

The critical filter has a very important function: It acts as an evaluator of the inputs/experiences/suggestions that pass through the conscious mind as we go about living. It then checks the database of knowns in the upper subconscious for the appropriate (automatic) response(s).

For example, if I was to suggest that you rob my bank, and that I could guarantee you wouldn't be caught, chances are your immediate, default response after critical filter evaluation would be, "No way!" because for most of us, robbing banks isn't acceptable behavior, so it's not a known. Another way to say it is that most of us are not suggestible to the idea of robbing a bank. Now, if you are one of those few people who has learned and developed a known that robbing banks *is* an acceptable behavior, you might take me up on the suggestion. (Please, if you are one of those folks, do not call me.)

As we age, the critical filter also becomes less porous or flexible. The pathways between the conscious and upper subconscious become more and more fixed, rigid, and narrow. We become less suggestible to new inputs/experiences/suggestions. Thus, it becomes increasingly more difficult to get any new information or knowns into the upper subconscious, and equally difficult to remove any already in place. We are becoming set in our ways.

The Process of Consciousness

The two major components of the mind—conscious and subconscious—can and do work very well together. For example, an experienced driver can drive a car with the subconscious automatically handling basic physiological functions as well as the myriad of procedural details involved in the act of driving—shifting, steering, accelerating, decelerating, stopping, and so on. Meanwhile the conscious mind can deal with the cognitive issues of watching the traffic, deciding where to get off the freeway, calculating how long the trip will take, choosing what route to follow, and so on. This complementary cooperation makes for a much more efficient and safer process.

The conscious mind also has the power to take over from the subconscious and exert control over our knowns, our default responses to events and suggestions. It can override the firing of a preprogrammed subconscious behavior—a known—as it is happening; the conscious mind can step in, stop it, and change the response.

Here's an example. Let's say you have ingrained a habit of reaching for food to relieve the discomfort of a stressful situation. (This is a very common known in our day and age.) You work at a very stressful job, and your impulsive habit at work translates into reaching for a candy bar in a bowl on your desk, especially whenever your phone rings and it's your boss. Now, you're sitting at your desk, and the phone rings; it's your boss. You automatically look to the bowl and reach for the candy. Your conscious mind has the ability to step in right then and stop the action: "Hey there, self. Stop! Let's not do this, we're going to lose 10 pounds, remember?" And so you consciously and purposefully put the candy bar back in the dish, and instead take a deep breath and center yourself as you reach for the phone. This ability offers us the wonderful capacity of free will, meaning we need not always be beholden to the automatic choices, behaviors, and responses of our subconscious knowns. But...and this is a very big "but"...

Being so much more massive (88 to 90 percent vs. 10 to 12 percent), faster, and therefore more powerful, the subconscious autopilot is quick to take over whenever the conscious mind is not aware or is sidetracked, and it is easily sidetracked. For many if not most of us this happens quite often, and for rather extended periods of time. In other words, when the phone rings, you begin thinking consciously about what it is your boss wants of you and the subconscious takes over; you automatically reach for the candy.

This is the primary reason that willpower, a completely conscious process, is so ineffectual for most people. So if in the past you have tried and tried and tried to change a behavior—for example, quitting smoking or losing weight—through conscious willpower, yet failed and failed and failed, you now know why. It's not a weakness on your part; it's the way our minds have evolved. You're simply stuck in your knowns, reverting back to running on autopilot.

Another way to think of the balance of activity and control within our minds is to say that with 90 percent of our mind being subconscious, we are running on autopilot about 90 percent of the time, running the learned, imprinted programs and behavioral patterns—our knowns—and for most of us, many of those knowns are disempowering and painful.

Think about this for just a moment: How often during any given day do you really *consciously* think about how you are behaving or reacting to the people and events you encounter in real time as they unfold? If you're honest with yourself, and if you're like most people, the answer is: not very often; you just react automatically as per the programming of your knowns, painful or otherwise.

Development of the Mind, Phase 3: Socialization

As time passes and as we move from the modeling stage into the last phase of development called socialization—ages 14 to 21 and beyond to full adulthood—the critical filter becomes even less porous or flexible. Neural pathways between the conscious and the upper subconscious become increasingly fixed and rigid. Figuratively speaking, these pathways through the critical filter become so fixed it actually weakens the ability of the conscious mind to override a subconscious "known" behavioral or emotional response.

To state it more simply, we become not only "set in our ways," but also very resistant to change, any change. Homeostasis has set in. So, even though we may consciously wish to break a habit or pattern, or rid ourselves of a limiting belief or behavior, and even though we consciously and logically know that eliminating the negative known would be of great benefit, we simply cannot get it done (see Figure 11).

Figure 11

M4: Socialization
THE FORMATION OF HOMEOSTASIS AND BEING "STUCK."

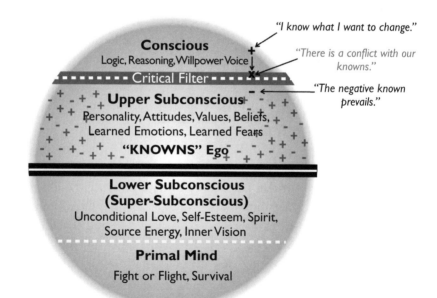

We are blocked; we feel broken, and it hurts. Even if willpower can force the issue for a while, it's almost as if there is a mental tug of war going on, with 10 percent of our mind (the conscious) pulling one way and 90 percent (the subconscious) pulling the other way. Who wins? We become the proverbial old dog that cannot be taught new tricks, and it is in this state that people such as Stacy find themselves: they are stuck, feeling isolated, despondent, and often a failure, constantly losing their internal tug of war.

It is the critical filter combined with the barrier blocking our connection to the tremendous and powerful energy resident in the lower subconscious (as shown in Figure 11) that prevents us from un-sticking ourselves. In essence, then, to affect lasting change as Stacy did, we have to find a way to get through or around the barrier of the critical filter, then help our 3-year-old upper subconscious, the engine of behavior, unlearn the limiting negative knowns, whatever they may be, and then learn new ones, the empowering ones we want to have.

In the process, we must also simultaneously unblock, or even better destroy the barrier between the lower subconscious and upper subconscious, thus reconnecting with the enormously powerful energy of unconditional love, self-esteem, and spirit, our higher and empowering energies, the stuff of the quantum web. As you will soon see, Synthesis can help fulfill and accomplish both these requirements.

⚹ ⚹ ⚹

While reading these last two chapters, you have very likely begun to look into your past and compared your personal experiences to what you now know about how your mind developed and how it works. You know how and why you think and behave the way you do. Thus, you have gained significant insight as to why you are feeling as you do and why you are creating and perpetuating a reality of disconnection. "I don't know," is no longer an appropriate response to the question, "Who am I and how did I get here?"

You now have a substantial part of the answer. You're getting to know *you* pretty well, both the part of you that is *you* and the part of you more reflective of *us*. We have also identified at least *what* must happen to begin to affect change and transformation. It is nearly time to bring it all together and discuss *how* to accomplish it with Synthesis.

There is, however, one final step in the process of your getting to know *you*, and that is to investigate the flow of quantum energy within you through a model that I like to call the human energy system. Knowing the relationship between our energies is extremely helpful in bringing the techniques of Synthesis into sharp focus, enabling you to create your desired changes as quickly and profoundly as possible.

CHAPTER 4 SUMMARY
Takeaways

⋊ The human mind is composed of two essential elements or layers: the conscious, and the far more powerful subconscious or unconscious, which work together to create consciousness, the essence of life.

⋊ The subconscious operates much like a computer hard drive; once it is programmed with knowns—engrained apps or patterns of thought, beliefs, emotions, attitudes, habits, and values—it will play these default programs repeatedly and automatically.

⋊ Knowns are formed through your life experiences, your connection to your environment, which includes both your immediate surroundings and the people within them, and also the cultural patterns and memes of society, or mass consciousness.

⋊ In the process of forming our knowns, most of us are cut off to some degree (often quite a lot) from the enormously powerful energies of the lower subconscious or superconscious: unconditional love, self-esteem, and spirit.

⋊ Creating lasting change in your life requires both conscious desire and unconscious reprogramming; creating new knowns and reconnecting to the superconscious energies in the lower subconscious.

Action Items

- How are your knowns affecting your life? In particular, take another look at the review you conducted around your beliefs. Are they Earth-round, or Earth-flat?
- Check your core values, which are also key knowns. Core values are the aspects of life that are vitally important and necessary to you. They are what I call the non-tradeoffs you *must* have in order to feel whole and secure. Earlier you were asked to consider whether you were living and acting according to *your* core values or someone else's. Now it's time to think seriously about what your core values really are. You might start with your career. What is important to you in your choice of career and position? What is it that you like about what you do? What is it that you don't like? The things you don't like often represent core values not being met. Some examples of possible career core values are teamwork, socialization, money, responsibility, independence, being of service, creativity, and flexibility. How about your core values for relationships? Some of these might be commitment, honesty, communication, intimacy, friendship, loyalty, and sharing activities. List your core values for your career and relationships, and then prioritize them, from most important to least important. (Least important does not mean not important, but there is always some hierarchy.) Once you have your lists, you can see where in your life your values are being met, and where, if anywhere, they are not being met. If you live in total accordance with *your* core values and you budget your expended energy toward them in the proper priority, the chances are very high that you are living a happy, productive, abundant, and satisfying life. If there are areas where you are not having core values met, or not in appropriate priority, or you are being forced to or are in any way trying to compromise on them, chances are you are living in disconnection. Change must create the ability for you to live your core values without compromise. Then the compromises that are a natural part of life are easy to make, as they are not central to your being.
- Imagine the mind in Figure 11 as the circle in the Quantum Reality Equation. What kind of reality would a mind in such conflict create? Remember the law of attraction. If you project the energy of

disconnection, conflict, and lack, you must attract it back, continually creating and perpetuating that reality.

❧ Continue your daily breathing exercises and continue opening yourself to the possibility for change, and, if possible, allowing your expectations for success to continue growing. You are paving the way for reprogramming your hard drive through Synthesis, with very powerful tools and techniques. You very well should expect great results, because if you use the tools, you will achieve the results you desire!

Chapter 5:
Magic Streams

Life engenders life. Energy creates energy. It is by spending oneself that one becomes rich.

—Sarah Bernhardt

As we discovered in Part I, one of the primary inaccuracies of the old Newtonian-Darwinian model describing our world and the essence of universal function is the concept of isolation and separation in the dynamics between and among energy systems and beings. A great example of this is the still prevalent conventional Western medical model, a model that considers and treats the human organism as composed of separate components, particularly wherein the mind and body are thought of as separate functional entities.

Quantum science demonstrates that all matter and everything in existence is simply the result of different expressions of the same Source energy, the energy of the quantum web, and we human beings are truly one of the most extraordinary, complex, and miraculous expressions of this energy. We are composed of the implicate energies of the mind—conscious logic and reasoning, the upper subconscious ego, and the superconscious spirit—and the explicate energies of the physical body, the vehicle that gives the mind a structure within which to reside and through which to experience the energy exchange of life on this space/time plane we call Earth. We now know that the mind and body, therefore, are inextricably connected—so, so sorry Monsieur Descartes!

The mind depends upon the body to conduct and deliver the energy of sensation and physical experience to the computer, the brain. In turn, everything that happens in and to the body, good and bad alike, must be processed by the mind through the computer, our brain. This complete interconnection and communication defines the human hologram, and it also means that the Quantum Reality Equation is just as viable in terms of producing physical reality as it is for mental and emotional reality. The mind, as represented by M4, is the nexus, the meeting place and interchange of our physical sensations and perceptions with our thoughts, feelings, and emotions producing the dynamic of belief, "truth," and ultimately our perceived reality.

The problem is that for most of us—at least in Western society—it doesn't feel that way. As our energy is invested and expressed in its different forms, each form *feels* like a discrete energy. Physical pain, for instance, feels like a distinct and separate experience from our thoughts and emotions. Of course, we all intuitively know and acknowledge that our different energies interact at some level; for example, experiencing physical illness or pain generally triggers negative thoughts, feelings, and emotions.

What many people do not understand, however, is that the opposite is also quite true: Negative thoughts, feelings, and emotions can also produce physical disconnection and illness. In fact, it has been determined that any given individual's perception of pain is more than 75 percent emotional in nature—which explains why there is such a wide range between individuals when it comes to their subjective experience and relative tolerance of pain.

Still, regardless of how our energy exchanges really work, we have to approach our work, creating physical, emotional, behavioral, and/or spiritual change in a way with which the average Western mind can relate, and in a clinical setting we must be able to accomplish this quickly; clients want and are paying for positive results. Thus, I developed the Human Energy System, a metaphorical model that combines quantum reality with how the processing and expressing of our various energies feels to us. The easiest and most practical way I have found is to consider and describe human energy as occurring in three distinct streams: physical, emotional, and spiritual, working through both the mind and body at the same time, and thus interacting with one another to produce our reality equations (see Figure 12).

Figure 12

The Human Energy System

The basic Human Energy System can be illustrated as three primary streams of energy.

Physical—energy of the cells and organ systems of the physical body
Emotional—energy of the ego; the conscious and upper subconscious
Spiritual—energy of the lower subconscious, superconscious; Love, Spirit, Inner Vision

The physical energy stream is the energy of the body; both the machinery, the structure—cells, bones, tissues, muscle, fibers, organ systems—and all physical sensations or feelings. Physical energy is ultimately, then, the expression of basic primal vitality, corporal health—wellness and or sickness—and all physical or kinesthetic sensations.

Emotional energy is the energy of "me," the individual you know as you, the person named Bill or Sue or Irving or Cathy. This is the energy of the cognitive conscious mind combined and interacting with the database of knowns in the upper subconscious—values, habits, behaviors, fears, beliefs, and so on. It is emotional energy that we feel and act upon most of the time, and of course, we now know that the ego, the "me," spends a lot of time on autopilot, running emotional and behavioral patterns of our knowns over and over again.

Spiritual energy is the energy of Source, your essence, your soul, the energy of the lower subconscious or superconscious. It is the energy of unconditional love, universal consciousness, inner vision, perfection, and divine wisdom. Spirit is the energy of inspiration, bliss, and creation itself; it is the very stuff of the quantum web. Most of us in Western society have lost contact with spiritual energy at some level or another, and that helps create the basic energetic imbalance—the Great Separation—that so plagues us.

With the model of the Human Energy System combined with M4 and the Quantum Reality Equation, we might describe the process of living, the human experience, as the result of consciousness—the mind—exchanging and processing energy through these three streams throughout a history that we call the lifespan; a fixed period of time from birth to death. In her wonderful book, *The Anatomy of the Spirit*, Caroline Myss describes this process as "biography becoming biology":

> As our lives unfold, our biological health becomes a living, breathing biographical statement that conveys our strengths, weaknesses, hopes and fears. Every thought you have has traveled through your biological system and activated a physiological response.... All our thoughts, regardless of their content, first enter our systems as energy. Those that carry emotional, mental, psychological or spiritual energy produce biological responses that are then stored in our cellular memory...our biographies are woven into our biological systems gradually, slowly, every day.[1]

We might also conclude that the degree to which our three energy streams flow, balance, and integrate (or not) in any given moment or period of time (or during our entire lifespan) determines the quality of our life experience. In fact, it is just this that Synthesis is meant to accomplish: the balance and integration of all three energy streams into a strong and unified flow. When this occurs, we have a healthy, happy, empowered being, creating a joyful reality. Likewise, when any or all three streams become weakened or out of balance, we experience disconnection—physical, emotional, and/or spiritual. As I mentioned in the Introduction, our disconnections almost always involve all three energies. We can consider them as distinct for the sake of simplicity and understanding, but in reality, they are as linked and interconnected as is the mind to the body.

To complete this model and make it more robust and functional, I also incorporate another concept: the theory of chakras, the seven distinct focal points or energy hubs arrayed from the base of the spine to the crown of the head through which the three energy streams are focused and flow. The concept of chakras originated in ancient Eastern cultures. It is a powerful meme in those cultures and has been passed down for more than 4,000 years.

The word *chakra* comes from Sanskrit and means "wheel" or "disk." Each chakra processes the expression and flow of physical energy in a localized part or system in the body, and also a corresponding emotional/spiritual energy. In terms of the emotional/spiritual energies, starting at the base of the spine and moving up, the lower chakras are the centers or loci for more primal or what we might call materially/ego-oriented emotional energies; the higher chakras are the loci for more superconsciously based spiritual energies.

Many clients have asked me why I incorporate the chakra concept into my models of the human experience. Here's why: Using the concept of chakras gives the energy model a definite visible structure, which I find appeals to our Western, "Let me see it" sensibility. Moreover, I also figured that if a concept or theory still exists more than 4,000 years after its inception, it's likely that there is something to it. And apparently there is!

Much like the ancient and seemingly accurate view of universal structure and energetic interconnection, there is more empirical, scientific evidence continually emerging that suggests that the chakras actually exist. There is also overwhelming evidence of a definite correlation between physical disconnection (disease) in various parts of the body and certain emotional and psychological conditions or energies, all emblematic of the concept of the mind-body connection as shown in Figure 13 on the next page.

Figure 13

The Human Energy System With Chakras

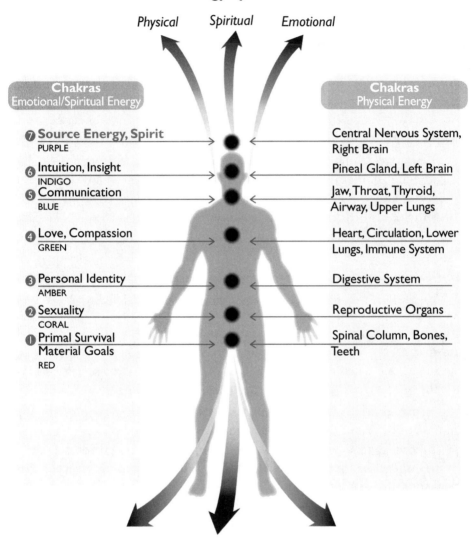

The three energy streams of the Human Energy System flow and are focused through seven focal points or chakras. Each chakra represents different physical and emotional/spiritual elements.

Some of the typically related physical and emotional/spiritual energies associated with each chakra, as well as their corresponding colors from the visual energy spectrum, are included here.

Another way to express this concept is to say that if an individual is experiencing a negative emotional or psychological energy condition—stress, anger, fear—and if that energy is not processed and resolved appropriately, and becomes chronic, the energy must be expressed *somewhere*. For us humans, that somewhere is our physical body. Sigmund Freud was one of the first Western scientists to study and write about this phenomenon. He called the process of converting strong emotions into physical illness "hysterical conversion." A more modern version of this theory, often called Body Syndromes by mind/body practitioners, correlates emotional/spiritual disconnection to localized areas of the physical body.

In time, if the emotional condition is not resolved, the physical response can become permanent, a chronic condition of disconnection we call illness. To take this a step further, there is abundant and growing clinical evidence that there is *no* physical illness that does not have a corresponding emotional/psychological indication or causal component, and these relationships often correspond to the location and particular energies associated with the chakras. Many writers, such as Carolyn Myss and Louise Hay, have researched and written quite extensively on this phenomenon.

A few representative examples of the quite common illnesses whose causes or etiology are definitely attributed to an emotional component—stress, anger, fear, frustration—would include: Irritable Bowel Syndrome or IBS, Lupus, Epstein-Barr, Ulcerative Colitis, migraines, Chronic Fatigue Syndrome, peptic ulcers, and coronary heart disease. The list also includes a variety of chronic pain conditions—neck, shoulder, back—and even cancer, which emotionally is most often associated with long-held and/or repressed anger and/or strong resentment. Throughout protracted time periods, this internalized energy eventually causes the body to attack and consume itself.

It should be no surprise that, given the emotional factor in the etiology or cause of physical maladies, many of them become generational; they run in specific races and in families. Think back to the concept of memes, cultural or familial thought patterns; emotional energies (beliefs) passed from one generation to the next. It is not a huge stretch to envision the negative emotional and physical tendencies for a given physical illness actually becoming literally infused into the DNA of a given population of people or a family line.

Also not so surprising is the fact that many or most of these conditions respond poorly to conventional Western medical protocols that still treat the body like a machine independent of the mind. "Take this pill and call me in the morning" often does not alleviate the condition well; sometimes not at all. Perhaps it is because conventional Western medicine is most often about treating and alleviating *symptoms* and not addressing the *cause* of illness: energy disconnection. In my view, as wonderful and powerful as Western medicine is, this is the single greatest weakness in its medical models and protocols.

Knowledge of the chakras and body syndromes and the correlation between the various physical illnesses and emotional energies can be very helpful in the clinic, particularly when a client comes in for help dealing with a physical condition similar to any of those just mentioned. The reason they seek help from someone like me is almost always because the conventional medical treatment they received has not worked to any great effect. Once I get the appropriate and required referral and authorization to work on the condition from their physician, we go to work at the cause—energy imbalance and disconnection—targeting all three energy streams to create healing and wellness in both mind and body.

Using all the models, but in particular the Quantum Reality Equation, M4, and the Human Energy System, we can sometimes quickly identify the specific triggering emotional issue for a physical ailment. Once (and if) the client processes and resolves the causative emotional energy (it isn't a given), and once we re-balance the three energy streams (in conjunction with conventional treatments), we almost always see significant symptomatic resolution, and sometimes complete relief. We create a new reality equation, physically, emotionally, and spiritually!

Of course, no treatment modality is perfect, and not all people experience successful outcomes. My theory regarding the reason for this focuses on the fact (as previously mentioned) that some of us learn to completely identify ourselves—our very essence—with and by our illnesses and disconnections. Once we're diagnosed and therefore labeled with a condition, it becomes us and we become it. I see this again and again: "I *am* depressed," "I *am* ADHD," "I *am* anxious," "I *am* IBS," "I *am* bulimic," and so on.

These people simply cannot let go; they cannot or refuse to acknowledge, process, and then release the negative emotional energy that is causing the physical malady. Doing so takes both dedication and effort, and to reiterate an earlier and salient point, many people in today's society are simply looking for the magic pill, the silver bullet, and instant results. Today we see ads everywhere that tout such solutions: "Want to lose weight? Forget about nutrition or exercise; just get a Lap Band procedure or liposuction!" "Want to quit smoking? Use our patch or chew our gum!" "Feeling anxious? We have just the pill for you!"

Although these procedures and medications may have an appropriate place for extreme conditions, many people have them and take them unnecessarily. Further, even measures as drastic as surgery do not always work. I recently worked with a man named Greg who had had *three* Lap Band procedures and was still overeating. In fact, he was eating more every day than he should have been physically able to fit into his constricted stomach. And I suppose not surprisingly, he was also still gaining weight. It was instantly apparent to me that no one had ever successfully treated the real causes of his overeating. Surgery simply cannot do that. Thus, the problem had never been resolved.

As it turned out, the cause of his eating addiction was a long history of maternal, emotional abuse, and a resulting severe, almost complete lack of self-esteem. People often overeat and allow themselves to become obese because the excess weight acts like a protective shield for a very fragile, insecure ego and negative self-image.

On the other side of this coin, more often than not, many of my clients do really, really well. I so love it when a client comes in or calls after a breakthrough session and reports that "My headache/backache/shoulder pain [choose your ache] is gone," or "I've been sleeping like a baby," or "No more stomach cramps," or "I've felt calm and in control all week, with no anxiety," or "I flew to Miami last week, no sweat!" Yippee!

It is in these moments when I affirm that the theory of chakras and physical/emotional/spiritual energy connections fit perfectly with the idea of Synthesis—blending the universal wisdom and traditions of ancient and indigenous tribal cultures with modern science and technology. We take the best of both worldviews and philosophies and help individuals tap into and manage their magic energy streams to create a better, healthier, happier, empowered life.

EXPLORING THE CHAKRAS

What and Where Are the Chakras?

The **first chakra** is located at the base of the spinal column, right above the coccyx or tailbone. This is the most primal energy center of the seven; it can be thought of as our connection to the basic structure and necessities of life, our connection to the Earth. Physical energy of the first chakra is associated with the spinal column, skeletal system, the teeth and nails, and organs of elimination. The emotional/spiritual energy of this chakra is that of basic survival, which for our forbearers was centered on obtaining food, shelter, and fire. In modern civilization, first-chakra energy is also attributed to material security—the attainment of goals in the material realm, stability, and grounding. The color associated with this chakra is red: bright, fiery, vibrant, and powerful.

The **second chakra** is located in the pelvic region, the site of our reproductive organs. Second-chakra energy is the energy of the sex organs—reproduction, fertility, and potency. The emotional/spiritual energy associated with the second chakra is that of sexuality, sensuality, primal desires, procreation, basic emotional needs, and relationships. Its color is coral: lush, corporeal, sensuous.

The solar plexus is the site of the **third chakra**. The third chakra is where we begin to see a transition from more primal, animal energies to more evolved, spiritual energies; or we might say from more simple, basic energies to more complex. Physical energy of the third chakra concerns the digestive system and organs—the liver, stomach, spleen, gall bladder, and pancreas. The emotional/spiritual energy of this chakra is concerned with personal power, formation of opinions, social identity, influence, self-control, and will. The energy of the transitional third chakra is where we cultivate the beginning of personal growth. The third chakra is represented by amber: warm, deep, intense.

The **fourth chakra** is centered over the heart. It can be considered the first of the truly "higher-energy" chakras. The electromagnetic energy of the heart is even more intense than that of the brain, and the heart is sometimes considered almost a second brain. Physical energy of the fourth chakra is focused on the heart and circulatory system, lower lungs, and the immune system, which is highly reactive and subject to great harm under chronic stress. It is not surprising that many of the so-called immune deficiency diseases, some of which were mentioned earlier, are associated with a high level of stress, as is coronary heart disease itself. The emotional/spiritual energy of the heart chakra is the powerful energy of unconditional love, and the complex emotions of compassion, tenderness, forgiveness, understanding, equilibrium, and transformation. Here we see the transition into the more evolved cerebral energies we associate with the spiritual realm of the superconscious. The fourth chakra is represented by green, one of the principle colors we associate with life on our mother Earth: clear, fresh, wholesome.

The **fifth chakra** is located at the throat, right over the thyroid gland, and is responsible for growth and maturation. The physical energy of the fifth chakra involves the jaw, throat, neck, the vocal cords, airway, and upper lungs—the apparatus of communication. Perhaps not surprisingly, the emotional/spiritual energy of the fifth chakra is the energy of self-expression and communication, independence, the flow of thoughts, and one's sense of security. The fifth chakra is represented by pale blue: cool, fluid, lucid.

The **sixth chakra** rests right above the eyes, in the center of the forehead. Physically, the sixth chakra is associated with the endocrine system, particularly the pineal gland, the gland responsible for secreting melatonin, which regulates our sleep and waking cycles. It is also associated with the left hemisphere of the brain. Emotionally and spiritually, the sixth chakra is associated with peace of mind, insight, imagination, intuition, and the balancing of the higher and lower selves. This is the seat of the guiding and protective energy, the so-called sixth sense, and inner vision; for this reason, the sixth chakra is often related to the concept of the "third eye." The sixth chakra is represented by dark blue or indigo: deep, rich, complex.

The **seventh** and highest **chakra** is called the crown chakra; it is located at the crown of the head. Physically it is associated with the right brain and the pituitary gland, which regulates the endocrine system and also connects to the central nervous system—the major sensory conduit for the entire mind and body. The crown chakra is associated with spirit itself—Source energy. This is the energy of perfection, universal consciousness, and divine wisdom and purpose. It is the gateway to the soul, the superconscious. The colors of the crown chakra, our connection to the quantum web and the energy of all that exists, are violet or purple: regal, sacred, divine.

Working With the Chakras

When working with and considering the chakras, one concept I find particularly useful is to remember that whereas each of the seven has a distinct energetic focus or purpose, it is the blending and integrating of the three energy streams comprising the Human Energy System through all seven chakras that produces a healthy, productive, empowered, and evolved being. Quite often, after I've finished working with a client on a specific issue or condition, our last session is dedicated to reinforcing this concept; we balance and integrate the energies of all seven chakras as our last exercise together. Never once have I seen someone leave this last session without the glow of a blissful smile and a little extra kick in his step. It's a great way to go about living this miracle we call life.

CHAPTER 5 SUMMARY
Takeaways

⊰ The Human Energy System creates a graphic depiction of our energy streams, as we perceive them: physical, emotional, and spiritual. We can visualize our energy streams as flowing through and focused by the seven chakras, each of which has a particular physical and emotional/spiritual component.

⊰ Our diseases—physical and emotional/spiritual—are almost always caused by some imbalance in our energy streams, usually all three. Creating change involves balancing and integrating our streams.

⊰ Combining all the metaphorical models—the Human Hologram, Quantum Reality Equation, M4, and the Human Energy System— is an excellent way to cater to our Western sensibility and provide a sense of empirical evidence; we can actually see and therefore better understand what is somewhat abstract and esoteric for most people. Understanding and knowledge are the precursors to using the tools of Synthesis powerfully and obtaining results quickly.

Action Items

⮱ Review all the action items you've been assigned thus far. Proceeding into the next section, you should have an understanding of the all the models to use as a basis for applying the tools you're going to be using. You should have a list of your core values for both your career/hobbies and your relationships, and each list should also be prioritized from most important to least important. Remember, doing so helps you determine which of your values are "must haves," and which you can compromise. It should have also helped you distinguish those values that are truly yours from those that others have told or expected you to live by, and *that* in and of itself is often the key to life-transforming change; just knowing and then living by *your* core values. You should have reviewed your belief system and listed your Earth-flat beliefs; those that are holding you back. Limiting or Earth-flat beliefs are usually easy to find; for example, "I'm not enough": worthy enough, smart enough, sexy enough, lovable enough, deserving enough, and so on. Bring the list with you as we proceed.

⮱ If you haven't done this yet, list the specific areas in your life where you are seeking change. Ask yourself this question: What is going to be different about me when I'm finished? Prioritize this list as well, from most important to least important.

⮱ How's your feeling of expectation? Are you beginning to see how you can take greater control of your life and experiences through knowing how you work and knowing the Quantum Reality Equation is mutable, that the law of attraction, although a physical law, can be manipulated? It truly can be.

⮱ Continue the daily breathing exercises, *at least* once a day, every day. Notice any differences in how you feel after the exercise. Pay attention to them.

Part III

From Theory to Practice: Creating a Better You

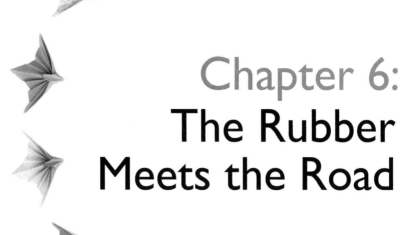

Chapter 6:
The Rubber
Meets the Road

In theory, there is no difference between theory and practice; in practice, there is.
—Yogi Berra

We have reached the beginning of the most important part of this journey together. We have built our foundation of theory and knowledge. We know how the "engine's" systems work now, and how we create our reality and our disconnections, both individual and societal. It's now time to use our models in Synthesis with some very powerful tools. We're going to shift from theory to practice, from thinking to thinking *and* doing. We are going to generate change, and create a new reality, a better you—whatever that might mean for you.

Creating significant and lasting change is where the rubber meets the road in human development. I believe—I know—that we all have the ability and the inner resources to do so. In fact, to settle for anything less would be a waste of the journey, a waste of the knowledge and understanding that you've come all this way to acquire.

Of course, even with the potential and power of Synthesis, we need be mindful of avoiding a vexing challenge: It's one thing to understand intellectually the hows and whys of getting into our issues and disconnections—as you now do—and quite another for most people to *do* something about it and have it stick. People who actually try to do something to change their lives most often find themselves slipping back into their old patterns and disconnections after a painfully short period of time. As we discussed earlier, the reason for this has little to do with personal weakness, and everything to do with the functionality of the human mind and four important, intrinsically related phenomena that result from that functionality. Let's review them.

CHANGING DISCONNECTION TO CONNECTION

First, most people in our society do not realize that they are actually creating their own reality. Because they feel and believe they are victims of circumstance, they are living "at effect"; they feel powerless to do anything about their issues and disconnections. They often identify with and become their disconnections; it thus defines their life experiences.

Second, for physical, emotional, and/or spiritual changes to really stick they must ultimately be created at a deeper level than that of our conscious mind, and that, of course, means at the subconscious level—the engine of behavior—home of the programmed and engrained patterns we call "knowns," the drivers of the Quantum Reality Equation.

Third, we know that due to the huge inequity in mass or power between the conscious mind and the unconscious mind (10 to 12 percent conscious vs. 88 to 90 percent subconscious) and the inertia of homeostasis created by the critical filter, the conscious mind alone is rarely powerful enough to do this. The conscious mind alone cannot tilt the scales of change in the subconscious and keep them tilted in the desired direction. After a time (usually a short time), the scales tip back and keep us stuck. After enough fruitless attempts to change by means of the comparatively weak force of conscious willpower, many people will just give up and decide to accept their life as it is. And "as it is" is often quite painful and limiting.

Fourth and finally, as a result of the seven deadly memes, including and especially the Great Separation, most people live in and suffer from some level of socio-emotional or spiritual isolation—usually both, and quite often to a significant degree. In fact, for many of us, the energy of the lower subconscious or superconscious becomes so obscured, we fumble and grind our way through life completely unaware of our spiritual energy stream; it lies virtually stagnant. This stagnancy creates a huge energy void within, which inhibits us from utilizing the predictive and protective power of inner vision, and it becomes a huge source of inner pain and disconnection. Being unaware of its cause, we often have not a hint as to what it is or what can be done to alleviate it. We live with this vague feeling of lack, an unknown emptiness. In desperation, many people turn to numbing activities such as substance abuse or behavioral extremes and addictions in an attempt to ease the pain and fill the void, none of which ever work.

So, whatever the issue and desired change, in order to succeed, we must ensure that we address all four of these areas. We must first change our attitude to be "at cause." Our attitude must be, "I created this reality of mine and it's my responsibility to create my new one; it is no one else's job or responsibility to make me happy, just mine."

We must work on and change the programming, the negative knowns in the upper subconscious hard drive, and we must find a way to ensure that the inertia of homeostasis does not reject and thwart our desire to create a better reality. And of course, we absolutely *must* end the isolation from our superconscious higher energies and create a strong flow, integration, and balance in and among the three magic streams of energy in our Human Energy System—physical, emotional, and spiritual; especially spiritual, the intelligent essence of all creation and the universal quantum web itself.

Succeeding With Synthesis

I have devised my version of Synthesis to address all of these concerns; it is a process that has helped literally thousands of clients accomplish their goals for change and personal growth, and I am going to guide you through it step by step. Along the way, I will introduce you to many of the same powerful models, tools, and techniques I use with my clients in the clinic and teach to other therapists who I mentor. You are about to discover exactly what you need to do to succeed in changing your life. (And by the way, if you've been accomplishing the action items presented in each chapter thus far, you have actually already begun the process.)

WHICH COMES FIRST?

As was the case with the metaphorical models in Part I: Foundations, and Part II: Getting to Know You, there is a continuing enigma, an ongoing conundrum of chicken-and-egg-ness involved in both introducing and describing the process of Synthesis, and also actually using the tools and techniques to affect it. I will introduce and discuss the various elements and techniques of Synthesis in a linear fashion, as the constraints of a book dictate I must. But keep in mind that in reality it's all happening at the same time. So I beg you, please bear with these constraints. I trust when we're finished you will see how it all fits together.

I must also forewarn you that some of the steps in this process will require you to examine yourself and your issue(s) with complete objectivity and honest self-appraisal. (Although it will probably be evident to you when this sort of objectivity is needed, I will make specific note of these areas.) Truly objective self-assessment is usually not an easy task for most of us. Nor is it any easier for our friends and families, people who are invested in our lives. If you do find yourself having difficulty performing an objective assessment where and when it's indicated, please, as tempted as you may be, *do not put the book down and give up!*

I will present techniques, tricks of the trade, so to speak, to help you over these hurdles if and when they occur, and that may be all you need. If it's not, if you still find yourself somehow blocked, or confused, or in any way in need of assistance with objectivity in self-assessment—I must trust that you will be honest with yourself in this regard—just go get some help with it, and then pick up the process where you left off. Uh-oh, I can almost hear the screams: "Get help? You mean, like, *I should see someone?* Are you nuts? Why do you think I bought this book? I don't want anyone messing with my head! Are you for real?"

Believe me, I understand this thinking. In most quarters of modern society there is a "mega meme," a giant cultural gene that attaches a significant stigma to the concept of seeking therapeutic assistance for mental health issues. *It's just not done*, is the thinking. But in fact, it's just not done *enough*. If more of us did seek appropriate professional help, we'd all likely be much better off. Consider this: How many of us grow our own food, fix our own cars, fill our own teeth, or fly ourselves across the country? Do many of us perform surgery on ourselves, catch our own fish, or sew our own clothes? Do most of us make our own shoes or build our own homes?

Clearly not; we rely on others for assistance with a myriad of life's necessities. Yet, when we have an emotional, habitual, behavioral, or spiritual issue that is causing us stress and disconnection, we feel as if we are supposed to be able to solve it all on our own, or somehow just suck it up. And then, if we cannot or do not suck it up, we feel even weaker or somehow more defective, which creates even more disconnection. Here's an example.

Several years ago, I worked with Steven, a successful entrepreneur in his mid-30s, who came to me for help overcoming chronic stress, insomnia, worry, and what he described as persistent low-grade anxiety. When we met for his first session, he told me that he had been referred by one of my clients. When I expressed my delight and asked how the client who referred him was doing, he informed me that he didn't really know; he had been referred *some five years prior.*

Naturally, I asked him why he had waited so long to come in. He relayed that he had been raised by parents whose motto and attitude concerning any challenging situation was, "Suck it up and act like a man." Thus, Steven grew to believe that to seek help for a personal issue would be to discredit his manhood and his parents' heritage. He said, "I've always figured I'd live with it and work things out the best I can." And of course, he suffered for it.

When I asked what had changed his mind, he admitted that he had recently been married, an event that had triggered the worst episode of worry, insomnia, and anxiety ever. He decided to call me and come in because he did not want to enter his new life with all his emotional troubles in tow. I congratulated him and we got to work.

Four weeks later, he came in for his weekly session and reported feeling worlds better. That week had been especially telling in terms of his progress; he had realized that his energy had shifted markedly. He was sleeping soundly and was ecstatic over a strong but unexpected uptick in his business; financial concerns had been among his primary stressors to begin with.

At that point I asked him whether he thought his business success was due simply to good fortune or to the fact that his energy had changed through our work together in reducing his stress, and the more positive outlook he felt with being at cause. I then showed him the Quantum Reality Equation—I had just formulated it—and explained the law of attraction. His face lit up. "I think I get this. Why did I wait so long?" That session turned out to be our last.

I have one word to describe this mega meme of "deal with it" and "suck it up"; that word is, *ABSURD*! If you need a little help, and this (or any) book isn't quite enough, then, damn it, go get it! You're worth it.

This is your life, and a happy, abundant, fulfilling life is your birthright! So get whatever help you need. There's just one caveat: I would avoid turning to a friend or loved one. You want someone who can be completely objective, someone who has no stake in the outcome of your experience except *your* success, health, and happiness—not his or her view of it. That someone is best found in a trained counselor or therapist, and I'll provide you some guidelines for finding a good one. (See Appendix B.)

Frankly, if in taking you through this process, I only get you far enough to realize you need more than I can give you in these pages, and you actually go get the assistance you need, then I will have succeeded admirably in achieving my goal for this book. And when you come back, this process will be even more powerful for you!

I would also like to begin this part of the journey with a gentle reminder as to the bigger picture: why we're here, what it's all about; the simple notion from whence and where we began. *Life is supposed to be fun!* Okay? It really, really is, and it really, really can be. I promise.

※ ※ ※

TWO DRIVERS OF SYNTHESIS

Two of the primary drivers behind Synthesis (including all the tools and techniques for generating change and creating a new and powerful reality) are the concepts of allowance and process. I liken both allowance and process to conduits for amplifying and streamlining the efficiency in the flow of quantum energy, thus producing change faster. We will consider both concepts in greater detail as we continue, but I am going to request that you think and consciously affirm, right now: *I allow the process* [it is a process and not instantaneous] *of changing my life to be fun. I enjoy it!*

Oscar Wilde once said something to the effect of, "Life is much too important to be taken so seriously." Seriously—pun intended—with the simple act of consciously choosing to let it be fun, you automatically start fulfilling the requirement to create balance and integration among your three energy streams. Please, say it again, right now: *I allow the process of changing my life to be fun. I enjoy it!*

In our very first session, I explain to every new client that the process of Synthesis, of changing and empowering your life, is really a very simple one. It can be easy or difficult for you, but it is absolutely simple. And you absolutely have the power and prerogative to choose your path, easy or difficult. I always suggest to them, and now to you: just choose and allow it to be easy.

So, let's add that concept to the first affirmation and we'll let this be part of your next takeaway assignment. Write the following statement down, read it aloud, and repeat it over and over, and over and over, and over and over. Say it with energy, mean it, and continue to do so until it feels natural to you: *I allow the process of changing my life to be fun; I enjoy it, and I choose and allow it to be easy!*

THE FORMULA FOR CHANGE

When working with any new client—and I now consider you a new client—I like to present a clear, practical, logical, and empirical picture to explain the hows and whys of universal reality and how we create our disconnection, and I like to establish an equally clear picture of the hows and whys of creating whatever change and transformation they (and you) desire. I have important reasons for doing so. Beating the proverbial dead horse just one more time, doing this fulfills the Western sensibility of needing to see in order to believe. Also, many of my new clients are skeptical at the outset of our working together. You may still be, too. They, and maybe you, feel they have "tried everything" to no benefit, so why should this be any different?

I figure if I can provide a tangible plan or blueprint, a definite structure around which to begin to create successful change, a hopeful notion forms, however faint, that maybe this time things will be different. "Maybe there *is* something definite and practical that I can do to finally begin to overcome what I wish to overcome." I call this plan, this structure, this something, the Formula for Change.

The Formula for Change was the result of an extensive review and analysis (part of the research for my doctoral dissertation) of more than 1,000 client cases, conducted throughout several years of clinical practice. The sample cases were chosen to represent a cross section of the issues I work with, from behavioral to habitual, from physical to emotional to spiritual, and just about everything in between. I also chose cases with different outcomes—highly successful, moderately successful, and unsuccessful. As I mentioned, the vast majority of my clients do well, yet not all cases work out.

My goal for this study was to identify and correlate any common denominators or combination of energies that seemed to produce successful case outcomes while likewise identifying what, if anything, was missing in cases that were only moderately successful, or worse, unsuccessful. In reviewing case after case, a definite pattern emerged that eventually suggested the formula for success. Figure 14 represents a graphic depiction of my Formula for Change, a simple, elegant, and very powerful energy concoction for initiating personal growth and development.

Take a minute to look at it on the next page.

As you can see from Figure 14, the Formula for Change is a combination of ingredients or energies—conscious energies representing various chakras in the Human Energy System—combined with two powerful accelerants or catalysts: intention and expectation. The initial ingredients and the catalysts *never* vary. It matters not an iota what the desired change entails; it can be physical, emotional, habitual, behavioral, or spiritual. It can even be a desire to overcome one's fear of and resistance to the only real constant in life: change itself; perhaps not surprisingly, this is an issue I work with a lot.

Regardless of the disconnection, the formula always applies, is always consistent, and always works when executed correctly in combination with the right tools. The tools must allow us to work with the subconscious engine of behavior. I prefer and primarily employ hypnosis and meditation, as they are both extremely powerful agents for change when used correctly. However, we always start with conscious energies, as it is the conscious mind that recognizes the reality and pain of contrast and disconnection in the first place.

As with any good recipe, the Formula for Change works best when you, the cook (so to speak), really know and understand the ingredients and the tools, and how they need to come together for your particular situation. Each individual brings his or her own combination of the required components, and therefore each individual has specific needs in bringing the ingredients and tools together to create an effective result.

Figure 14

The Formula for Change

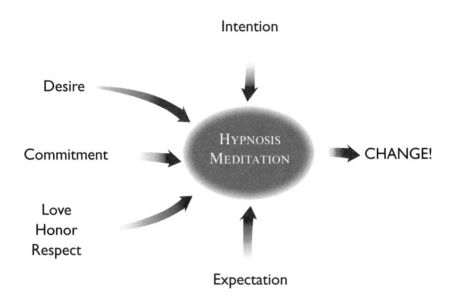

The ingredients (conscious energies) for initiating and creating change are consistent regardless of the nature of the change an individual seeks. The blending of the ingredients with two powerful catalysts, intention and expectation (also conscious energies), accelerates the process, generating the necessary momentum to initiate the desired change.

The circle represents the spiritual and subconscious energies that, through the tools of hypnosis and meditation, coalesce with the outer conscious ingredients into the energy of change and transformation, creating new knowns and a new reality.

I like to leave nothing to chance. Thus, in the clinic, we always begin by discussing each of the formula's components and together determine what's needed in terms of nuance and emphasis so as to produce a mix of energies that best suits the individual client. We'll begin that process for you in the next chapter. I will define and characterize each ingredient and then describe the specific considerations and requirements that need to be considered in its use. You will then assess how you stand in relation to that ingredient, as well as any adjustments you need to make for your particular situation and issue. Once we build your personal version of the formula, we'll explore how to engage it in combination with the therapeutic tools and some ancillary techniques so as to co-generate the magic of Synthesis in the subconscious, and, ultimately, create your new reality.

CHAPTER 6 SUMMARY
Takeaways

- In creating change, we switch from theory to practice. Our examination of history, anthropology, and science, as well as the models—the Human Hologram, Quantum Reality Equation, M4, and the Human Energy System—give us our foundations. Now we build upon them and begin the process of manipulating our quantum energies to create a new reality.

- Our process for changing requires an awareness of the challenges we face due to the functionality of our minds. We must be "at cause"; we must reprogram our subconscious hard drives; we must end the Great Separation, and create balance among all three energy streams in the Human Energy System.

- There is always a chicken-and-egg syndrome at work. Pay it no mind whatsoever.

- To succeed in changing your life, you will have to be able to assess yourself objectively. This may be difficult; do not be afraid to seek help if you need it.

- Change is a process; there are no instant fixes.
- Life is supposed to be fun! Allow the process of change to be fun and also easy.
- The Formula for Change is a recipe of conscious energies and catalysts blended with spiritual and subconscious reprogramming using powerful tools to stimulate and generate the creation of your desired change.

Action Items

- It is time for you to ensure you are choosing to be "at cause," taking full responsibility for creating your own reality and for creating changes in it.
- Continue your breathing exercises—21 slow, deep, and gentle breaths at least once a day, every day.
- When you finish your breathing, begin to recite the affirmation on page 139: *I allow the process of changing my life to be fun; I enjoy it and I choose and allow it to be easy!* Repeat it until you feel it! When you feel it, it becomes a real energetic vibration projected into the universal field, which, of course, you must attract back. It is law.

Chapter 7:
Made With Only the Finest Ingredients

You don't have to cook fancy or complicated masterpieces; just good food from fresh ingredients.

—Julia Child

I used to love Julia Child's cooking show, *The French Chef.* The show would always open with Julia standing in front of her cooktop and prep table, and in her inimitable, booming voice, she'd welcome the viewers and announce the project of the day. "Todaaaay, we're going to look at a wonderful and delightfully flavorful recipe, one of my favorites...," after which she would immediately describe the dish, list the ingredients, and then dive into the cooking.

Well, now it's my turn. Todaaaay, we're going to look at a wonderful and delightfully flavorful recipe, the Formula for Change, one of my favorites, resulting in an empowered and happy, joyfully engaged you—creator of health, wellness, peace, and abundance, whatever you desire, the reality of your dreams! And here are the ingredients we need to get you started; nothing fancy or complicated, just simple, fresh, and very powerful!

DESIRE: YA GOTTA WANT IT!

Actor and political commentator Ben Stein said it well: "The first step to getting the things you want out of life is this: Decide what you want." Thus, your formula for changing your life begins with the most elemental and freshest ingredient imaginable: deciding what you want. Then you just need the desire to make it happen.

Deciding what you want is, of course, a conscious process. Even though we ultimately need to work at and within the deeper levels of the upper and lower subconscious, the conscious mind must initiate and then *actively participate* in the process. Synthesis is all about integration, balance, and harmony on every level, including the two components of your mind; the conscious informs and guides the subconscious.

Desire is created through contrast; you feel a lack or overabundance of some energy, you do not like it, and begin to want the opposite. It may seem blatantly obvious that, without your desire to have it occur nothing can or will change, but it is critically important to ensure that the desire to change is in fact *your* desire. You must make certain that this is something you want for *you* and not because someone else—a friend, relative, or loved one—wants it for you, or thinks you should have it and/or will be the better for it. I'll remind you once again of my client Tim, the law school graduate who "couldn't" pass the bar exam. He "couldn't" pass because what he really wanted to be was a chef, not an attorney. He was trying and in a real way being forced to compromise his core values, his true self, for the expectations of others. It bears repeating that this never works, at least not for the long term and/or not without a great deal of pain and disconnection.

I get quite a few calls from people who say they want to make a change in their lives, and when I ask them why, they hesitate for a moment, and then admit that it is because someone else in their life wants them to and thinks—or worse, *knows*—they'll be better off when they've done it. Who can possibly know what's best for us better than us? The answer is, no one, but how they try to convince us otherwise, and me oh my, to our detriment, how often we listen.

I also receive a lot of calls from people who call *on behalf* of a friend, loved one, or child because the caller wants the friend or loved one or child to change something that the caller finds displeasing or distasteful. Several years back, I received an earnest call from an apparently frustrated husband who, "at his wits' end" asked me to do hypnotherapy with his wife to make her want to have intimate relations with him again!

In these situations, I almost invariably and rather quickly discover that the friend or loved one or child (or the aforementioned wife), whomever the intended client is, is perfectly happy just as he or she is and really does not wish to change a thing. I *never* take these cases. If your conscious desire for change is not conceived "of you, by you, and for you," the chances for a successful outcome are slim at best. As Bill Cosby said, "I don't know the key to success, but the key to failure is trying to please everybody."

So, step one: Identify the desire and make sure it's yours.

Next, you must begin to define your perception or vision of the successful outcome of fulfilling that desire as best you can; in other words, as specifically as possible. How will you know when you've achieved it? What will you feel like when you have it? How will you look and behave? Your clear concept and/or vision of the outcome will be extremely important when we begin our deeper subconscious work, so it's best to begin working on that part as soon as possible; it may take some time and several iterations to crystallize it fully.

Prioritizing

If you have a list of several (or what may seem like many) changes you desire to create in your life—and this is not at all uncommon—simply list them in priority from most important to least. You want to work on one issue at a time. A scattergun approach is inefficient and counterproductive and will often serve to derail you. Remember, the conscious mind, which plays a big role in all of this work, is designed to focus on one thing at a time, and this is especially important when creating a change in your life. Prioritizing is important because I want you to begin with the most important issue. Once you have constructed your list, imagine that each issue is like a stone in a pyramid, with the most important issue at the very the top or peak of the pyramid.

Next, imagine turning the pyramid upside down. When you do this you place the most important issue on the bottom, but now the entire structure of your pyramid, your list of disconnections, is resting upon that number-one issue. Now, consider this: If that stone is knocked out of the pyramid, what happens to all the others? Of course, they will fall; the pyramid will collapse upon itself. In other words, eliminate the most important source of your disconnection, and all the other issues become much less significant and much easier to overcome. They often and quickly turn into little more than metaphorical mosquitoes in the tent of your life; you will likely be able to virtually flick them away, or *Whack!*, squash them dead.

Self-Assessment Alert

One last and very important thing to check after you list your desired change or changes is whether you can identify the underlying known, the causative emotional energy or limiting belief behind the issue. If you have a list of issues and changes, is there a common emotional issue or limiting belief at the root of all of them? I find this is very often the case with clients.

Recognizing the causative knowns—emotions, limiting beliefs, and so on—and eliminating *them* rather than just dealing with the behavioral symptoms' manifestation/s alone makes the whole process of change quicker, more efficient, and lasting. And similar to envisioning the outcome, this serves to begin engaging the subconscious mind in the process; it is, after all, from within the subconscious that these knowns arise. Finally, if you identify the limiting, causative knowns, it also strongly assists you in verifying and solidifying your desire to get rid of them.

To assist you in this activity, I'm going to present examples. We'll take a look at two common issues that I deal with regularly, with which I think most people can identify. First, we'll look at the symptom—the behavior—and then take a peek under the hood and outline some of the knowns that cause and perpetuate the behavior.

Example #1: Smoking

In any given year, I work with between 50 and 150 people who want to quit smoking. As a behavior, smoking is pretty straightforward. An intelligent and supposedly rational human being, purposely, repeatedly, habitually inhales hundreds of incredibly toxic chemicals into his or her body, sometimes as many as 40, 60, or more times a day, every day, 365 days a year, year after year, quite often in the guise of obtaining pleasure and relaxation. Many people call and say, "I want to quit, but I so love smoking."

That's the behavior, and we all know it's one that can and will kill you. In fact, when you think about smoking from a strictly behavior-vs.-outcome perspective, you have to wonder why anyone would actually do it. It seems rather insane, don't you think? So what's behind this insanity?

If you ask them, most smokers will immediately blame their physical addiction to nicotine for not being able to quit—a notion that the pharmaceutical companies hawking their very expensive pills, patches, and gums love to perpetuate. I do not dispute that nicotine (which by the way is a natural insecticide for the tobacco plant) is an insidiously addictive substance. Having once been an addicted smoker, I can attest to that fact with aplomb.

But I also know from my personal experience, and more importantly from having helped hundreds of people stop smoking for good, that the underlying emotional issues and limiting beliefs about the habit are far more responsible for perpetuating both the addiction and the behavior itself. In truth, for most people the physical pain of nicotine withdrawal is quite minimal, often physically painless, and it's usually over within 72 to 96 hours after you stop smoking.

Yet I repeatedly see people who quit "cold turkey" agonize for weeks, months, even years afterward, and worse, they often subsequently substitute some other self-destructive behavior such as overeating for their smoking. Why? Well, they stopped doing the behavior, but they didn't address and resolve the underlying emotional issues—the knowns—that led them to become and then stay smokers in the first place.

So let's take that peek under the hood of the smoking behavior. Every individual is, of course, unique, yet there are several common patterns of knowns or underlying causes behind the smoking habit and addiction. These include social insecurity, a desire for acceptance, lack of stress-management skills, a rebellious streak, low self-esteem, a tendency for self-destructive and self-sabotaging behavior, hopelessness and frustration with life, sexual fetishism, feeling unworthy or inferior, and believing the popular and seemingly universal meme that quitting *must* be hard.

These emotional issues and limiting beliefs can and do appear in various combinations, and they can also quite often appear in other areas of an individual's life as well, and thus contribute to or cause other problems. So imagine what happens when someone comes in to quit smoking and we actually address and neutralize both the behavior *and* the emotional issues and limiting beliefs creating the behavior. First, quitting becomes not only easy, but also painless! Further, successfully resolving the actual causes of his or her smoking habit very often leads to a desire to create other life-transforming changes; the inverted pyramid begins to tumble, and they happily begin to flick away the mosquitoes in their tent!

Example #2: Overeating and Obesity

Another issue I work with on a regular basis is weight control. I guess there is no surprise here; obesity is epidemic in America. People eat too much of the wrong foods and lead very sedentary lives. Now, the natural way to lose weight is quite simple: burn more fuel than you ingest. In other words, change the behavior: eat better and move more. That's it, nothing more to it. Why then don't (or can't) people just do it? Because there are almost always underlying knowns that created the propensity to become and stay overweight or obese to begin with, and until addressed and resolved, these knowns preclude choosing to eat well and move more. Let's pop open the hood and take a look at obesity from within.

Some of the more common emotional issues and limiting beliefs behind chronic overeating or obesity that I repeatedly see in the clinic include low self-esteem, feeling unloved, fear of intimacy (where the weight acts as a protective shield), chronic guilt, chronic stress, lack of self-discipline, chronic anger, frustration, and fear of loss of control. Once these issues in whatever combination they appear are adequately resolved, making the choices of eating well and moving more becomes not only easy, but also compelling.

I've seen this transformation occur over and over again, and I've seen it happen in as few as two sessions, with a resulting loss of more than 85 pounds of unwanted and unhealthy weight. Resolve the emotional disconnection and healthy choices become compelling and natural; the weight melts away, easily and relatively effortlessly. It's really almost a secondary effect of what I call *learning to be chronically very kind to you*—not indulgent, necessarily, but very kind. As I like to say to my clients, we don't do weight loss, we do self-kindness.

⁂ ⁂ ⁂

The bottom line here is that there is always an important underlying known (or knowns)—emotional energy and/or limiting beliefs—causing every unhealthy, negative, or unwanted habit or behavior. These knowns must be processed and resolved in order to create change that is successful and lasting. And again, the same holds when dealing with multiple issues; there is quite often a common thread of negative knowns underpinning the whole list.

By taking the time and effort to objectively identify the underlying knowns behind your disconnection, you can get to the real heart of the matter and thus have a much better chance to succeed in changing your life for good. One way to accomplish this objective analysis is to suspend all self-judgment. Whatever is, simply is. You may not like it, and that's okay, but it's not good, or bad, or stupid; it just is. Choose to allow it to be nothing more than that. (There's that concept of allowance again.) Remember, it's all just energy and all energy can be transformed.

COMMITMENT: I CAN, I WILL, I DO!

I can, *I will*, and *I do* are statements of commitment, which is the second ingredient in our formula or recipe for change. Whenever I begin working with new clients, I let them know even before our first session that they must enter the process with a firm commitment to the work, which means a firm commitment to themselves. Commitment is associated with third-chakra energy, the source of our personal power and will.

Your commitment must be strong and unwavering: "I will do whatever it takes to make this happen. I will let nothing stop me, period!" This statement implies that the process will entail effort, and it does. There is no magic involved, but with the right commitment and the right tools, transforming your life can seem magically easy as well as simple. And remember, it *is* always simple; whether it's easy or hard is always your choice, and you already know how I feel about which choice you would be best served by.

The key point here is that you must know that this is *your* process. No one can change your life for you. You may be guided through the process and introduced to the tools and techniques, but the actual process of change is yours; you do the work, you create your new reality. I can tell you from vast experience, both my own and of all the people just like you with whom I've worked: Whatever effort you expend will be well worth the results you achieve. There is little more that need be said in this regard; if you consciously and conscientiously commit to the work, and to yourself, you must succeed. If you do not, you probably will not.

LOVE-HONOR-RESPECT: ALL YOU NEED IS LOVE

The third ingredient in our formula for change is actually three in one: love, honor, and respect—for yourself. To succeed in creating change and transformation, you must love, honor, and respect yourself; you must become (and therefore treat yourself as) the most important person on the planet.

This is not to say that you ought to become an egomaniac, or vain, or selfish, or narcissistic. What I mean is that you must enter the process committed not only to succeeding, but also to treating yourself very kindly. You commit to consciously, purposefully making choices that serve your growth, well-being, and the greater good, and to do so consistently. That means your choices in life become both self-empowering and what we call "ecological." Dr. Sheila Foreman, a Los Angeles–based psychotherapist and a colleague coined the term *self-fullness* to describe treating oneself in this manner. I like that idea quite a lot.

In our society we are generally not taught to love, honor, and respect ourselves very much or very well. In fact, most of us experience quite the opposite. Almost from the day we're born, there is someone (sometimes many someones) telling us that we are less than, not enough, or unworthy. As you no doubt remember from M4, with enough repetition, this sort of input or suggestion becomes a default, a known, and contributes heavily to our becoming blocked from the bountiful unconditional love, self-esteem, and spiritual energy we are all born with.

I don't think it is an exaggeration to state that virtually every emotional, behavioral, and/or spiritual disconnection that we experience involves a lack of self-love, honor, and respect to some degree. After all, if we *did* truly love, honor, and respect ourselves, we would likely not engage in the disconnected behavior or self-deprecation to begin with. Thus, we face a real chicken-and-egg moment here: We need an ingredient for our formula, the very lack of which is actually causing the needing!

How do we get around this conundrum? Do not despair. I've not met many people who have completely lost the ability to love, honor, and respect themselves; it isn't likely that you have lost it completely, either. Consider this: The very fact that you even want to make a change in your life, that you're reading these words, tells you and me that indeed, you still have the instincts for self-love, honor, and respect; otherwise, you wouldn't want to find a way change to begin with. In other words, the desire to change and a willingness to commit and simply begin the process is in and of itself an act of self-love, honor, and respect.

If that knowledge is not enough to get you going, if you are one of those people who truly feels unable or unknowing how to love, honor, and respect yourself, or that you do not deserve to feel that way—a nasty and very negative known and limiting belief—I offer the following exercise. We'll use a little good old-fashioned Western thinking: "I'll believe it when I see it," or what I like to call the "show me proof" technique.

Prove It!

Ask yourself this question: *Where did I learn that I was unworthy or unlovable? Who taught me?* Your answer may be *Mom,* or *Dad,* or *my first husband,* or any number of people. Consider whomever it was for a moment, then ask this question: *Who gave him, her, or them the right, authority, or certification/ qualification to sit in judgment of me, to evaluate me in terms of my worthiness or lovability?*

If you're honest with yourself, you will immediately realize that those people gave it to themselves. There is no certification committee or board to certify a person to judge another person for worthiness or lovability or lack thereof. They anoint themselves, and *we let them do it!* Okay, so maybe when you were a little kid you had no choice in the matter; you were completely suggestible and naïve. But now you *do* have a choice. You don't have to believe them anymore!

I once had a delightful and very energetic client named Zandra who, after several sessions, was still having trouble with letting go of these sorts of limiting beliefs, instilled in her when she was a little girl by what she described as an abusive mother who had always devalued and degraded her. She just could not seem to allow herself to let go of her mom-induced low self-image. It was really impeding her progress. One day, completely exasperated, she cried, "John, it's like the second I think about feeling good about myself I have these little voices in my head that start reminding me that I'm worthless."

A little frustrated, I quipped, "You know what? Fire them! You hired them; they're your voices, so just fire them! Tell them they are no longer needed and be done with them." Zandra looked at me a little startled, and then laughed herself to tears.

"That's it; just like that?"

"Why not?" I asked.

The following week she almost bounded into my office, such was the spring in her step. She was a different woman. I asked her how she was feeling.

"Awesome!"

"Oh?"

"Yup; it's all good! I did just what you said; I fired the bastards."

We were off to the races.

It's not unusual to hang on to these limiting thoughts and beliefs, these little voices or inner demons, for a very long time. But remember, as an adult, you *can choose* to listen and believe them, or not. If you do choose to believe them, then I charge you to find the proof, the empirical evidence that substantiates them. Show me; I'll believe it when I see it! Of course, you cannot, because there is no proof. That means the opposite must be true: You are absolutely deserving and lovable.

Here's another technique that works really well. Ask yourself, *Is this limiting thought or belief I have about myself Earth-round, or Earth-flat?* If it's Earth-flat, if there is no basis in fact for the thought or belief, you are believing a false truth—you are busted! As I rhetorically asked earlier, who wants to live an Earth-flat reality, one based upon false truths and therefore so limiting? Choose the Earth-round reality, the factual thought, to believe: We are all—and this includes you—equally worthy and deserving, and we are all equally lovable.

If for some reason even after this exercise you still believe that a negative, unloving thought or belief about yourself is true, take it another step. Ask yourself another question à la the wonderful work of Byron Katie. Ask yourself, *must* this thought or belief about me be true? If you are truly honest, you should realize that indeed, it doesn't *have* to be true, and if it doesn't have to be true then it was indeed Earth-flat and bogus all the while. Thus, you can choose to begin focusing on what you know *must* be true: its opposite.

Now you too can fire the negative inner voices. Or better, keep them on staff, but change their job: The inner voices can now be responsible for saying something such as, "I am worthy and lovable just like everyone else, so I think I'll start treating myself that way." Ah, now that's Earth-round! What we need to do now is strengthen that thought.

ADDING THE MAGIC

The very good news in that regard is that in engaging the Formula for Change, by consciously wanting change, choosing to commit to the process completely, and choosing to treat yourself with love, honor, and respect, you automatically do so. You begin to reconnect with the innate higher energies of unconditional love, self-esteem, and spirit in your lower subconscious or superconscious. You need these energies to help you destroy the disempowering knowns programmed into your upper subconscious that caused your disconnection in the first place.

It's worth repeating that even though we're looking at this process linearly, all this conscious and unconscious thinking happens at the same time; there are chickens laying eggs and eggs hatching into chickens all over the place!

Once you've begun to change your thinking, I liken the process to pushing a little snowball over the crest of a hill. As the snowball begins rolling down the hill, it builds both mass and momentum. Then we make the "snow" wet and sticky, causing it to get bigger faster by adding two very powerful catalysts to our process. A catalyst is defined as an agent that provokes or speeds significant change or action. In the Formula for Change, our catalysts, or what I like to call "the magic," are the energies of intention and expectation.

With intention and expectation working through your conscious desire and commitment, all in the spirit of love, honor, and respect—your self-fullness—the snowball of change grows formidable quite quickly. And soon, the process of transformation becomes unstoppable, and your new reality is essentially a fait accompli.

Intention

What is intention? In his book *The Power of Intention*, Dr. Wayne Dyer considers this question, ponders several possible answers, and finally likens the energy of intention to the creative energy of the universe itself—the God-force or universal energy field; that which we are calling the quantum web. Other writers on the subject express similar views. This is not at all a far-fetched idea when we consider that the universe is still growing and expanding. Worlds, perhaps even other universes are still being created at every moment, and according to quantum science, there seems to be intelligence in the energy of the quantum web, in the essence of universal structure; the stuff of all those new worlds, our world, and us.

So we could say then that intention may well be the most powerful energy or motive force in the entire universe. It is energy derived from all seven chakras. Nothing can be created without it. An artist cannot create art without it; an athlete cannot compete without it; a student cannot learn without it; a business cannot profit without it; a writer cannot write without it. Without intention, nothing can happen. It is the bridge between desire and creating a result.

Because we're in the process of creating a result—a better you—intention is a necessary catalyst. Yet for many people, especially we Westerners, defining *intention* as the creative force of the universe is a bit too abstract a concept to easily integrate and employ. We desire something more practical and pragmatic. So let's try this definition: **Intention is laser-sharp focused thought and action dedicated to producing a result.** The result in this case, is whatever you wish to change, your new you.

Let's take a look at this definition more closely. First, notice that two energies must be brought to bear here: We need to employ both thought and action. If you have either one without the other nothing much happens. Many of the latest books and films dealing with quantum reality and the law of attraction mention the necessity to focus one's thoughts on what one desires, but they most often minimize and sometimes completely neglect the need to act on those thoughts as well. We can chalk that up to Hollywood, I guess, but we're talking reality here—your reality. If you don't *do* something to take you through the process—choose, act, and so on—then, to borrow yet another old cliché, "You can't get there from here."

It's true; thought without appropriate choices or actions to further it produces nothing. Conversely, action without thought guarantees little more than a random chance for success at best. However, if you combine these energies with appropriate focus, you *must* create a result, and that result will be the one you want and can be expressed in any or all three of the human energy streams, and in any or all seven chakras.

The degree of focus becomes very important in producing efficacy. Think of light energy: photons. A light bulb does a fine job of projecting a fuzzy ball of photons and illuminating a room. But if you concentrate and focus those photons, they become a beam, brighter and sharper. And if you continue to focus them enough, that very same energy—light—becomes a laser, incredibly more powerful than any light bulb.

The same holds true for our intention and the process of change. The more we focus and concentrate our thoughts and actions on our desired outcome, the more quickly and efficiently we can and will produce the result.

Interestingly, the tools we will employ for harnessing and focusing the energy of the subconscious mind and reprogramming our knowns have just that effect: They produce extremely sharp focus and clear concentration, and thus more power in the vibrational energy of our thoughts, our desires, our commitment, and even the love, honor, and respect we show ourselves. In turn, the actions necessary to give form to the thoughts become much easier and more natural to accomplish, and the result—empowerment, personal growth, and transformation—must occur more quickly.

Expectation

Expectation is the other very powerful and necessary catalyst in utilizing and engaging in the Formula for Change. We discussed the energy of expectation earlier—yet another chicken-and-egg scenario—but it is worth reviewing here, for now you will see how expectation is employed in the grand scheme, so to speak.

When we begin to expect to see our result, we actually begin to tap into our innate ability to manipulate the energy of the quantum web, as verified in innumerable scientific studies in which thoughts or expectations for a result actually influenced what should have been a random outcome, creating instead the result that was expected or desired. The power of expectation (and intention) is also demonstrated in those amazing instances when individuals cure themselves of diseases, some even diagnosed as terminal, without medication. Expectation is apparently also the motive energy behind the placebo effect, whereby people derive the medicinal benefits of a drug when they in fact ingested a sugar pill. The energy of expectation is associated with the sixth chakra. It is the magic energy ingredient in all manifestation and the creative process. It is the force behind a lot of lucky people, too.

Most of us know someone, or at least know *about* someone who is naturally lucky. These folks are the individuals who always seem to get what they want, who seem to glide through life effortlessly, always smelling like the proverbial rose, ending up on the right side of the coin. Well, part of the reason for their innate good luck is that they *expect* to be lucky, and their expectation, projected along with their desire, commitment, and the focus of intention, is returned to them. To them it's natural, and they simply employ it regularly; they're the "lucky ones."

By consciously infusing expectation into our process, we in fact begin to "believe in order to see," rather than having to see in order to believe. We begin to think in the "old ways," which apparently is what really must occur in order to control and create our desired outcomes. Quantum energy responds to energy, and expectation is energy.

Now you can understand why one of your first action item assignments was about creating and entertaining even a tiny amount of expectation for your results. I dearly hope that as you are gaining ever more understanding of the process, your expectations for a successful outcome are growing. By allowing your expectation to grow stronger, by believing in order to see, you will—you must—begin to see what you wish to believe. As that occurs, your Western sensibilities begin to kick in; you are now seeing and thus more easily believing, and then believing more in order to see more, and then seeing even more in order to believe even more, and then believing even more in order to... And on it goes!

You are building a perpetual motion machine of creation powered by the vibrational alignment and projections of your quantum energy. When appropriately focused and strengthened it is manifested and returned to you through the law of attraction. Like a tiny seedling at germination, Synthesis is beginning to emerge.

Take another look at the Formula for Change.

Figure 15

The Formula for Change

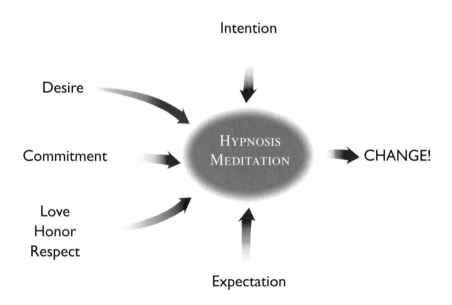

Intention

Desire

Commitment

Love
Honor
Respect

HYPNOSIS
MEDITATION

CHANGE!

Expectation

Engaging the conscious energies and catalysts in the formula initiates the process of change. However, as we saw with M4, our model of the mind, creating lasting change, requires that we bring these conscious energies to bear at a much deeper level, within the subconscious mind, the engine of behavior, as signified by the oval. It is within the subconscious that the real magic of Synthesis, what I call the "alchemy" of change and transformation, occurs.

Alchemy is defined as a power or process of transforming something common into something special. We know it is quite common for people to live in chronic disconnection, and it is something oh so special to transform, to heal, and to rise from the ashes of that disconnection like a phoenix, a creator of health, wellness, peace, joy, and abundance. So for me, the term *alchemy* is apt.

We are ready to go to work inside the oval, so to speak, to give the engine of behavior a much-needed tune-up and service. To do so we need a way in, a set of tools or a methodology that can bypass the built-in resistance of the critical filter and homeostasis, that will allow our seedling of Synthesis and change to burst forth, take root, and thrive.

I once wrote in a paper (and still maintain) that there is no one methodology absolutely required for the process of Synthesis. Any protocol that recognizes and embraces quantum reality, that operates through the focus and manipulation of energy, and that creates a positive change in the energy interaction between an individual and his or her environment—and thus a new reality equation—can be viable.

Still, after spending much of my adult life in research, study, and experimentation, both for my own growth and for that of my clients, I have found no other methods or tools for accomplishing and maintaining this objective that are safer, more natural, more powerful, or more profoundly effective than hypnosis and meditation. Hypnosis and meditation are really nothing more than states of mind or consciousness, yet when purposefully engaged in conjunction with the power of the conscious mind, they are, as we shall see, truly one of nature's greatest gifts to humanity.

CHAPTER 7 SUMMARY
Takeaways

▹ The Formula for Change represents the conscious energies we use to begin the process of change and prepare for our work in the subconscious realm to eliminate unwanted knowns and establish new ones. There are three primary conscious "ingredients" or energies in the formula: desire, commitment, and the tri-partite love, honor, and respect for oneself.

- Desire: You must begin with a desire, and it must be yours.
- Commitment: You must commit fully to yourself and the process.
- Love, honor, respect: You must treat yourself with absolute and unconditional love. Treating yourself as the most important person on the planet establishes self-fullness, a condition wherein your choices are empowering and ecological. In giving yourself the gift of love, honor, and respect, you also connect into the higher energies of your lower subconscious; energies that are needed to create and maintain personal empowerment.

⇥ Catalysts (accelerants) for the Formula for Change are intention and expectation.

- Intention serves to define and focus your energy and ensure you act upon your thoughts, an absolute requirement for success.
- Expectation allows you to tap into the old ways, into the realm of quantum reality and the manipulation of quantum energy, which in turn triggers your Western sensibilities; you believe in order to see in order to believe...

Action Items

⇥ Identify and clarify your desire for change, and make sure it's really yours and not someone else's vision for you. If you have a list of things to change, prioritize them from most important to least, then visualize turning them over to form an inverted pyramid.

⇥ Begin to picture, visualize, or imagine—whatever works best for you—what your outcome will be like; the more clarity you can bring to bear, the better. We cannot create what we cannot imagine, so this is really important.

⇥ If possible, identify the cause of your unwanted known/s. Where and when did you learn this negative or unwanted feeling, behavior, or limiting belief? By identifying the cause, you can usually more quickly expose it for the false or Earth-flat untruth that it really is. If you cannot do this, it's okay, but if you can, it's very helpful in accelerating the process.

⊰| As you do this work, choose to suspend all self-judgment; just allow it to be what it is—unwanted energy—and let it go. Remember love, honor, and respect for yourself; these must be at work to succeed.

⊰| If you are having difficulty finding and giving yourself love, honor, and respect, and you are hanging on to self-denigrating thoughts or limiting beliefs, use the techniques outlined on pages (153-155). It is important to remember that you have the choice to think whatever you wish about anything, including yourself. Remember, *everything* you think, do, say, and feel requires a choice. Most of our choices are subconscious and therefore automatic (and maybe negative), but this is your time to engage your conscious ability to override the negative knowns and defaults and start the process of creating new, empowering ones. You're "at cause" now, so remember, the Earth is round! Think Earth-round thoughts; make Earth-round choices as much and as often as possible.

⊰| Continue your breathing exercises, 21 slow, deep, and gentle breaths *at least* once a day, every day. When you finish the breathing, continue to recite the affirmation, *I allow the process of changing my life to be fun; I enjoy it and I choose and allow it to be easy!* Add the affirmation, *I am as worthy and lovable as anyone and everyone; I am treating myself that way every day in every way.* Similar to the first affirmation, repeat this, perhaps even looking in the mirror, until you feel it. Intend and expect it, thereby focusing the vibration of this incredibly powerful energy, and allowing the universe to do its part.

⊰| Focus your intention and expand your expectations for your outcome as much as possible; you cannot over-intend, nor can you over-expect that you will realize the result, as long as you remember that you are in a process that must run its course. There is no magic, instant fix, but the more you intend and expect, the more quickly the process can proceed to its desired end, and the more quickly you can move on to your next adventure.

Chapter 8: Alchemy

Change is the constant, the signal for rebirth, the egg of the phoenix.
—Christina Baldwin

Michaela leans all the way back in my recliner, focuses her attention on a spot on the ceiling above, and begins to breathe slowly, gently, and deeply. As she does, I begin speaking to her quietly, soothingly; I suggest to her that at some point her eyes are going to start blinking either more quickly or slowly than they normally do, and that with each blink she can let her eyelids feel heavier and heavier until on one of the blinks they simply want to stay closed, and she'll allow them to do so.

As Michaela's eyes close, her eyelids begin to flutter rapidly but gently, indicating a shift in consciousness, the onset of hypnosis. Her breathing grows soft, gentle, and rhythmic, and I remind her that she can now allow her body to release any and all remaining physical stress and tension.

Her body is growing as relaxed and comfortable as her eyes, which I suggest are now so heavy and comfortable that they simply will not open, no matter how hard she tries. I ask her to try to open them and find that they will not.

As she tries and, just as suggested, finds they will not open, I remind her how wonderful that feels and suggest that she now release into even deeper comfort, calm, focus, and ease as I count down; "Five and deeper, and four and deeper still, and now completely releasing at three, two, one, zero; deep sleep."

At the suggestion "deep sleep," Michaela's lower jaw drops slightly; she breathes a tiny sigh, and with it, releases the last little bit of physical tension in her body. Her head turns and almost flops gently to the side as her neck muscles completely loosen. Beneath her eyelids, her eyes now appear as if she's looking up toward inside her forehead. She looks as if she is indeed sound asleep.

Michaela is not asleep; she has entered a deep hypnotic trance; her body is now completely relaxed, as limp as a rag doll. She knows it's there but she cannot feel it. Her mind is clear and acutely focused; she can hear every word I say. She knows she could open her eyes and instantly come out of trance if she wanted to, but she does not; it feels so very nice to be there. It is time for some alchemy; she's about to fly to Las Vegas!

※　※　※

NATURALLY HYPNOTIC EXPERIENCES

Hypnosis is a natural state of consciousness that every normal human brain voluntarily experiences every single day. The operative words in that last sentence are natural, consciousness, and voluntarily. And when I say every day, I do not exaggerate. Consider the following questions: Do you ever get so engrossed in a good book that you cannot put it down? Do you ever daydream? Have you ever been driving and suddenly realize that you're way past your exit, or find that you are pulling up to your office when you were really on your way to an offsite breakfast meeting? Do you like to play and become engrossed in video games? Do you ever watch a movie or TV show and find yourself laughing, crying, or feeling excited or terrified?

If you answered yes to any of those questions, you've been hypnotized. Almost all of us experience these naturally hypnotic moments all the time, beginning in early childhood and continuing throughout our entire lives. In fact, between the ages of about 2 and 6, kids actually spend most of their waking moments in a highly suggestible, essentially hypnotic state. When we recall the fact that during that period of life the upper subconscious is in the process of being imprinted, or essentially programmed, recording inputs/experiences and suggestions and creating knowns, this fact probably isn't so surprising. Anyway, let's go back to the movies.

What happens when you watch a good movie? When the lights go down you are automatically "guided" to focus all your attention on the screen; you "forget" the distractions around you. Soon you are experiencing the story as if you are living it yourself. The tension builds—Wait. No! Don't do it—don't go in there!!!

Okay, let's hold the phone here; is this movie real? Of course, not; a bunch of people played make-believe and a bunch of other people photographed it. You are watching the images—light and shadow projected on the screen at 24 frames per second—of their game of pretend, and intellectually, consciously, you know it; it's really a double illusion.

But a good movie entrances—hypnotizes—you. Your subconscious mind takes over from the conscious mind, and because it cannot distinguish between reality and illusion, for those two hours the experience you perceive and the feelings and emotions you feel are very real indeed. Entranced, you respond to the "suggestions" of the story. Then, when the movie ends, the lights come up and you come out of hypnosis, back to conscious awareness and into real "reality."

Of course, if the movie is a stinker you are not hypnotized by it; you do not go into trance, you do not respond to its suggestions; you probably instead sit there wondering how anyone ever got the money to make such a horrible film. Maybe you simply leave the theater, wishing you had believed the reviews and not cousin Bobbo.

When most people think of hypnosis, they do not think of naturally hypnotic experiences such as watching movies or daydreaming; they think of a stage show where they've seen a group of volunteers get hypnotized to perform a variety of silly, inane, and what many would deem embarrassing stunts that certainly no one "in their right mind" would ever consider doing. The obvious conclusion is that the hypnotist has taken over, and that the poor saps have lost control of their minds. In reality, nothing could be further from the truth. Remember the operative words in the first sentence of my description; voluntarily was one of them.

The volunteers in the stage show are up on the stage because they want to be in the show. They also happen to be among a very small percentage of the population at large who are able to enter hypnotic trance both quickly and profoundly. A trained stage hypnotist can find these folks in the audience—that's always the very first part of the show—and they become his or her subjects.

Once these wannabe showmen are hypnotized, they happily do all the goofy stunts, and sometimes equally happily even forget they did them. Hypnotic amnesia is not at all uncommon for people very adept at hypnosis, which these folks are. Of course, no one is ever asked to do anything immoral or dangerous, or lewd. If they were, they would likely come out of trance instantly and indignantly, and the show would be over. Worse, if the distasteful suggestion was not antithetical to their morals or values, they might actually do it—and the show would still likely be over.

The point is that no one can be forced or guided to do anything that is against their morals, values, or desires. This is another reason why any desire for change in your life must be yours and not someone else's. Using hypnosis or not, if it's not your desire, if it's not in accord with your core values, it won't stick, period.

Given that hypnosis—trance—is a natural state of human consciousness, it is just as naturally as old as we are. And because it is only that—a state of consciousness—once it's induced, it can be employed in a variety of ways. Besides its obvious application for entertainment, hypnosis has also been in use as a therapeutic and medicinal tool for more than 7,000 years, literally since the dawn of civilization. As I mentioned earlier, if something has been in use for that long, there must be a reason for it, and there is: It works!

Open to Suggestion

When we enter a trance state, our minds become very flexible and receptive to suggestion. The sensation is very similar to what happens to us in our naturally occurring hypnotic moments such as when we go to the movies, except in a clinical setting, we bring it to a much deeper and more profound level—exponentially more profound. This creates the perfect state of mind for accomplishing what we know we must in order to create lasting change.

If you recall from the mind model, M4, in order to reprogram the sub-conscious hard drive (create new knowns) we have to overcome homeostasis, our natural resistance to any change, even change we want and know is highly beneficial to us. Overcoming homeostasis requires bypassing the critical filter. Hypnosis creates just such a state of mind. When we enter a hypnotic or meditative trance the critical filter actually shuts off, allowing direct contact between the conscious and upper subconscious.

With the critical filter out of the way, our mind becomes almost child-like; open and receptive, much like it was when we were very young, before the critical filter had even developed. We can communicate directly with the subconscious and give the upper subconscious, the 3-year-old, some much-needed new direction. And like any 3-year-old, it will believe whatever we tell it. We can also further eradicate the barrier between the upper and lower subconscious—now from within—and thus reconnect fully to our powerful superconscious energies, which may have been lying long forgotten and dormant in the lower subconscious.

Then, when we come out of hypnosis and the critical filter "turns back on" (we actually need it in order to function and survive), when it receives the conscious input for change, and checks the database in the upper subconscious, instead of seeing a conflict it sees alignment; we've planted the seeds of change deep within (See Figure 16 on the next page).

In short, hypnosis opens and frees the mind. It allows us to fully utilize and integrate all the conscious energies and catalysts we generate with the Formula for Change—desire, commitment, love-honor-respect, intention, and expectation with absolutely no resistance. This helps us to essentially unlearn the unwanted, negative, unhealthy, and harmful knowns holding us back, and then to re-learn new ones, the ones we want. With both parts of the mind in energetic alignment, the internal tug of war between what we want and how we are programmed comes delightfully to an end!

⁂ ⁂ ⁂

M4: The Mind Before Hypnosis
(HOMEOSTASIS)

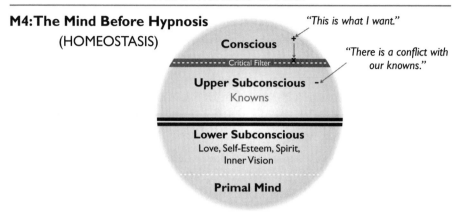

M4: The Mind in Hypnosis

Figure 16

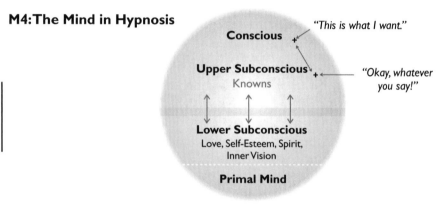

M4: The Mind After Hypnosis

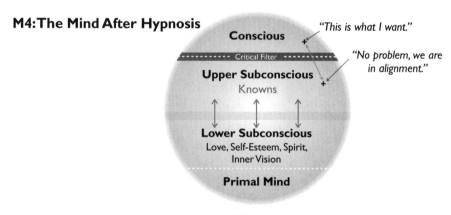

MICHAELA GOES TO LAS VEGAS

Today's session is Michaela's fifth weekly session. We've been working to eliminate what had become a crippling fear of flying, and it is my hope that today is graduation day for her. After four weeks of sessions and daily home-work exercises, Michaela is very comfortable with and adept at entering a deep trance, so I begin by reminding her how deeply relaxed she's feeling, and how in this state of total ease and relaxation she is also feeling wonderfully calm. I remind her that she created this state and can do so at any time she chooses; she's always in control, always alert, aware, safe, and very, very calm.

I then to guide her to her "special place," a place she's created in her mind, her own little kingdom. The special place is like a mental workshop, laboratory, and sanctuary. It is a place of absolute beauty, peace, and safety. When she's in this place, she can do anything, subject only to the limits of her imagination.

Once she is inside her place, I have her imagine stepping into a circle on the ground; we call it the circle of safety. Then, I have her imagine closing her eyes. Next, I count down from 5 to 0, which further deepens her trance, and at 0, she visualizes opening her eyes to find herself in her home and packing for a trip to Las Vegas.

I ask her to "live" the experience as I describe it. In deep hypnosis, it will feel real to her. It's sort of like watching the best movie ever made, except in-stead of watching the movie on a screen (a technique we sometimes use), she is actually associating into the experience. In other words, in her mind's eye, she is "living" the experience, "seeing" it through her own eyes, and incorporating all her senses, so also feeling it as it unfolds.

Image and imagination is in fact the language of the subconscious. George Bernard Shaw said, "Imagination is the beginning of creation. You imagine what you desire, you will what you imagine, and at last you create what you will." In essence, we think in images, and therefore, when we use image and imagination we are "speaking" to the subconscious in its own language. And again, when we're in hypnosis or trance, there is no critical filter to say, "No, this isn't real; let's reject this nonsense and listen to our knowns!"

As we proceed through the experience, systematically, starting from the moment she packs her bag to the moment she walks out of the terminal at her destination, I ask her to try to find that old fear, reminding her that she is in complete control, calm and safe, at all times. I suggest that to her delight, she will have great difficulty finding that old feeling. I also remind her to use a prearranged signal, unconsciously raising her right forefinger, if at any time she somehow does find herself feeling her old fear. This is called an ideomotor response, and serves as a way for her to communicate with me without disturbing her trance.

As I say, "You look out the window of the taxi and notice that you are approaching the entrance to the airport," she abreacts (a term for the expression of a negative feeling or emotion); her body stiffens and her right forefinger begins to rise. Immediately, I have her dissolve the image and find herself back in her place, in the circle of safety, feeling completely calm, relaxed, and in total control. I remind her that she is always safe and in total control and that she will find it ever more difficult to experience any other feeling except calm, centered control when I next count down, and bring her back into the scenario.

We re-enter the scenario just prior to the moment she felt the fear—approaching the airport entrance—and continue. This time she makes it all the way onto to the airplane, with no adverse reaction. As I describe the "aircraft door closing," Michaela abreacts, but only slightly. Still, I take her out of the scene and back to her place, once again reinforcing her feelings of deep calm, ease, and total control, and then we go back into the scenario. This time she abreacts at the moment of takeoff, although her reaction is tiny. Nonetheless, we repeat the cycle again. On the next iteration, she makes it all the way to Las Vegas. I now have her repeat the entire scenario from the beginning and she is able to "experience" the entire trip with complete calm and nonchalance.

I end the session by reminding her that, moving forward, the harder she tries to find her old fearful feelings, the less she will be able to find and feel them. They have been and will henceforth be replaced with this wonderful feeling of calm, ease, safety, and control, and she will allow this feeling to quickly blossom into a true fondness for flying anywhere at any time. I then guide her out of trance with a slow count to 5, and watch her smile and excitement broaden with each number as she returns to full conscious awareness.

For most people, hypnosis feels incredibly and profoundly pleasant; a very nice, natural high, and never is there any hangover. Such is the case for Michaela, even though she's been working pretty hard for the last 30 minutes. At "5," her eyes open, she brings the chair forward, looks at me, and exclaims, "I believe I am ready for takeoff!"

I assure Michaela that I too think she is indeed ready for the real deal, a flight to Las Vegas for a business conference scheduled for three days hence. Before she leaves, I remind her to continue her homework, which includes a daily meditative exercise to reinforce our session work and strengthen her ability to create and maintain focus, calm, and control of her feelings at all times, especially whenever she will be flying.

※ ※ ※

MEDITATION IN SYNTHESIS

Meditation and hypnosis are different terms for nearly identical states of consciousness. As such, they have a very similar, almost identical effect on both the mind and the body. They are so alike in both feeling and effect that in my opinion, the terms can basically be interchanged. The chief difference between meditation and hypnosis, if there is one, is not so much in the state of mind and body that they produce, but rather in the intended goals and expectations usually associated with their use, particularly as reflected in the philosophical traditions they are most identified with.

Meditation is most often linked with indigenous and Eastern cultures that were founded on the concept of constant change, a search for relationships, and the idea of seeking to understand and live as an interconnected part of a greater whole or system—what we've been referring to as "the old ways." Meditation is meant to be a long-term practice and systemic in its application. It is traditionally associated with achieving enduring goals such as serenity, peace of mind, and spiritual enlightenment.

Contemporary Western thinking, of course, is simpler. We tend to concentrate on the salient, isolated parts of the system, with much less or little regard for the whole and the big-picture interrelationships generated by the parts. Hypnosis and hypnotherapy are usually more associated with this Western ethos—treating particular issues, and individual parts of the whole. People seeking hypnotherapy are generally most interested, at least initially, in achieving a specific outcome such as eliminating a symptom, emotion, habit, or, in Michaela's case, a fear or phobia.

Consider the concept of Synthesis—harnessing the knowledge of quantum reality, blending ancient wisdom with modern science, the conscious with the subconscious, and the integration and balance of all three energy streams through all seven chakras in the Human Energy System. In other words, Synthesis is about considering both the parts and the greater whole. So does it not make perfect sense to bring both modalities to bear?

This was a question that I pondered several years ago, as I was first contemplating the idea of Synthesis and developing my models. We know that creating change requires changing the mind. The process of erasing old knowns and creating new ones also entails consistent reinforcement, and usually this means repetition—we have to break the old neural circuits, create new ones (hypnosis is great for that), and then entrain or solidify them so they become long-term, hopefully permanent. As a long-time and regular practitioner of both self-hypnosis and meditation (they feel virtually identical to me), I realized that daily self-hypnosis/meditation might be the perfect way to accelerate this process in my clients.

As an experiment, I began to assign dynamic meditative exercises as homework to all my hypnotherapy clients, regardless of the issue we were working on. There are several forms or variations of meditation, each with specific benefits. Dynamic meditations are in essence highly focused and personalized visualizations of a desired physical or emotional state, condition, or process; direct communication with the subconscious mind using its own language, visualization, and imagination. Can you say self-hypnosis?

The assignment was simple. I would have the client take some time at least once every day to enter a light to medium state of trance (a state very easily taught and accomplished), then visualize themselves as having finished their hypnotherapy program, as having achieved their goal, whatever it might be. I never mentioned the word meditation, lest they have any preconceived misgivings or bias against the concept. I simply called it homework, or daily quiet time.

Clients were instructed to stay with the visualization until they could "feel" the energy of that new state of being, until they could say, "Oh, yeah, that's it, that's what I want to be, how I want to feel." Once they could "feel" the energy of the vision, I knew their subconscious mind was responding to the autosuggestions it was giving itself: "I have succeeded; this is the new me, and I like it!"

Almost immediately, I noticed a substantial increase in the efficiency of my programs, across the spectrum of issues that clients came in to work on. This was how Synthesis really began. Today, depending on the client and his or her issue and needs, I assign a variety of meditative exercises for homework. And today, my clients tend to complete their programs in about half the number of office sessions it used to take before Synthesis. I know the use of self-hypnosis/meditation has played a big role in creating that efficacy.

Some of the clinically proven benefits of regular meditation include inner calm, increased focus and concentration, reduced stress, decreased feelings of anxiety and depression, higher energy levels, increased creativity, improved memory and recall, greater happiness and self-esteem, improved physical and mental health, and greater overall awareness. This list of benefits is extremely similar to one you might see regarding the clinical benefits of therapeutic hypnosis.

In truth, though, given their Western proclivities, most hypnotherapy clients do compartmentalize; they feel that they're coming in to erase a particular symptom or emotion, or to change one aspect of their life, via the traditional hypnosis model. Yet, as discussed previously, in order to ensure a successful outcome, there is almost always an underlying systemic issue to be dispatched as well, and there is always reinforcement required. And too, is there anything on that list of benefits that a person would not want more of in his or her life?

Given the traditional association between meditation and long-term and systemic goals, a regular meditative practice is also a wonderful way for my clients to maintain what they've accomplished working with me, and also create even more change and personal growth on their own. Think of the inverted pyramid of issues we discussed earlier; knock out the keystone, the single issue holding up the pyramid, and the rest become mere mosquitoes in the tent of life. Self-hypnosis and dynamic meditation, basically one in the same state of mind, are wonderful mosquito swatters!

STRENGTHENING THE SPIRITUAL STREAM

To attain true and lasting health and wellness, we must balance and integrate all three energy streams in the Human Energy System. A strong spiritual stream makes it both easy and compelling to maintain balance in the physical and emotional streams, to keep the body healthy and the ego appropriately controlled and in check. The opposite, however, does not hold true. Physical and emotional energies cannot alone strengthen the spiritual stream.

So how can we strengthen the spiritual stream? After many years of exploring the human condition and various philosophic traditions, I believe the masters who hold that a regular and consistent meditative practice is the only really effective way to connect to, nurture, and strengthen that most vital of our three energy streams.

The energy we call spirit is the energy of pure consciousness, our essence, what we might term the God force within us. It is part of and connected to the energy that moves through all things, the energy of the quantum web itself. Stephen Covey stated it perfectly when he said, paraphrasing French cleric Pierre Teilhard de Chardin, "We are not human beings on a spiritual journey. We are spiritual beings on a human journey."[1]

Your spirit is also known as the greater part of you. An easy way to think about it is to imagine a sock puppet. When you put your hand and arm in the puppet, only a small part of "you" fits into the sock. Similarly, only a small part of your spiritual body, your spiritual energy or being, actually fits into your physical body. The greater part remains nonphysical, connected to Source, the Creator, the quantum web.

Like it or not we are all spiritual beings, and to restate an earlier point, it was Western society's unwitting abandonment and neglect of spirituality—the Great Separation—that became possibly the most damaging of the seven deadly memes that underlie and perpetuate the endemic disconnection we face today. It is through directly connecting to our spiritual energy stream that we ultimately and finally annihilate the barrier to our superconscious energies: unconditional love, true self-esteem, and one of our most powerful and (for most of us) long-forgotten faculties: inner vision.

TUNING IN

Just what is inner vision? Suppose a baby deer loses its mother. If it has been weaned from her milk, it has a very good chance of survival. It "knows" how to find food and shelter, and it "knows" which of its fellow creatures in the forest are harmless and which are to be avoided. It senses and automatically avoids danger. This instinctive protective "knowing" is inner vision, and it is common to all the sentient creatures on the Earth.

This includes us humans, as evidenced by the indigenous tribesmen I referenced earlier. When the great tsunami struck Indonesia and the Indian archipelago several years ago, similar to the wildlife in the region the tribesmen were somehow forewarned and were able to escape safely to higher ground, while thousands of "civilized" people, domestic companion animals, and livestock perished. They could not sense or connect to inner vision, could not foresee the impending threat, and paid dearly for it.

The reason for this phenomenon is that through the joint effects of the Great Separation and the hubris of our material and technologically based culture, we in modern society have forgotten who we really are, along with our natural connection to nature, the Earth, and the quantum web. We now look to outside influences to find and define and value ourselves. Obsessed with the world of the material, we tend to rely solely on our five physical senses—sight, hearing, touch, taste, and smell.

Lao-tzu, the ancient Chinese philosopher and author of the Tao Te Ching, said, "At the center of your being you have the answer; you know who you are and you know what you want." Inner vision is an extension and manifestation of our spiritual energy, a connection to the center of our being, the greater part of us—our soul—that is both timeless and in possession of all the wisdom and knowledge from everything it has ever experienced, perhaps throughout many lifetimes. It is a protective and even predictive intelligence that involves the perception of energy at a higher vibrational frequency than the other five senses. It is our true sixth sense, one that our indigenous brethren and the wild creatures still connect to and depend upon for their survival and safety.

Of course, we all still have moments of inner-vision clarity; those occasional "gut feelings" or hunches that then actually manifest are perfect examples of inner vision at work. For most of us, however, these moments occur at best only occasionally and are often not dependable. This is because we are constantly bombarded by interference from the world outside ourselves, the noise and static of mass consciousness and rampant ego, all obsessed with the material, and claiming to know what's best for us better than we do ourselves.

This does not have to be the case though. Inner vision can be strengthened and the signal purified through simply developing and strengthening our spiritual energy stream—something anyone can do. All it takes is a little consistent practice; going inside, quieting the mind, shutting out the outside "noise," and then learning to tune in and listen to, see, or feel—however you best perceive it—inner vision's guidance. Everyone has his or her preferred way of processing sensory information. How can we best quiet the mind and tune in? The only way I know is through regular meditation, what Tom Brown, Jr., calls "the Sacred Silence."[2]

Once purified, inner vision must and will always give us good guidance. Unlike your ego, your soul cannot lead you astray; when you are tuned into a strong signal, you can depend upon it for help in making empowering choices and decisions. Those synchronicities and hunches come more and more often and become more and more reliable. And you can go as far with developing and refining your inner vision as you wish.

You have the ability and potential to become as adept as the tribesmen are, and learn to sense the energy changes within the quantum web itself. It is simply a function of the degree of time and effort you have available and are willing to dedicate to practice. Truthfully, reaching that level entails an investment of significant time and effort, but it is very doable. At the very least, a daily period of quiet meditation will allow you to develop your inner vision into a powerful guide for your everyday life. It's inevitable; the more you learn to trust and listen to your inner wisdom and its guidance, the easier it becomes to do so, and the easier it becomes to do so, the more you will want to develop it, and then the more reliable it becomes, and so on—yet another perpetual motion machine of creation.

CONNECTING WITH NATURE

One of the best places to practice and refine inner vision is in nature, as far away from civilization as possible. Remember, the energy of nature is a perfect reflection of the quantum web; there is no contrast and no ego out there; it exists in perfect harmony and balance, and so presents a perfect spiritual classroom. And even in major urban environments such as New York or Los Angeles, there is almost always access to wild or natural places in the form of parks, and thus a way to connect to nature.

With regular practice, particularly surrounded by the perfection of nature's energy, your intuition and awareness will grow exponentially; this includes not only your inner-vision but the acuity your other five senses as well. You can learn to move without a sound and mask your energy field so you essentially become invisible in plain sight, much like the Native American scouts could do; you blend into the landscape so that even the wildlife forgets you're there, and then you can and will see some amazing sights.

My wife and I have made this a sort of hobby. We love to go to the woods to connect to spirit and hone our inner vision. When we have enough time in the woods to really fine-tune, we can hike a trail and "feel" other people's energy long before we hear or see them. And we delight in watching them walk right by, never noticing us even though we are sitting or standing in plain sight right at trail's edge. These moments are a wonderful reminder of just how unaware, distracted, oblivious, and disconnected to their surroundings most people are today.

As I mentioned, sitting or standing very still and with very quiet energy, blending into the landscape, so to speak, provides an opportunity to observe nature and wildlife in its natural state—not running away in terror from the scary humans noisily crashing and banging through their home. One day, while sitting next to a stream, I watched as a gopher snake leisurely crawled out of the woods, daintily took a drink of water from the stream, and then went casually on his way, never once recognizing my presence. A few moments later a hummingbird halted in mid-flight and hovered for nearly 30 seconds, inches in front of my face, seemingly just checking me out; it was an incredible moment, and we've had hundreds more like it.

We also love to "play" with the wildlife. We know a place in a local state park where a herd of deer regularly comes to feed. We find a good spot, usually under an old coastal live oak, and then sit very still and quiet our minds. When the deer arrive and begin to feed, we see how long we can stay "invisible" to them, and how close we can get them to come. Or, once they start grazing, we'll suddenly focus our attention upon the nearest individual. Through its inner vision, the animal instantly feels the energy, the attention; her head pops up and she becomes skittish; she looks and listens, searching for the source, but because we are so still she can't see us. We then "switch off" the focus and she soon settles down and goes back to grazing. This little energy game can be repeated over and over again, although sometimes the deer become agitated and leave. If ever one needed proof of the existence of this incredible faculty, these moments provide it.

For us, a day spent in the woods and these moments of energetic interaction are absolutely joyful, and also very powerful in keeping us able to tune in when we return to the world of civilization. There isn't a day that I don't consult inner vision several times for guidance and insight in making choices. It guides my work in the clinic and my life outside. Inner vision is a big part of Synthesis, and something every client learns about during our work together.

How far you take your work with inner vision is up to you, but at the very least, you owe it to yourself to get back in touch with this powerful internal guidance to help you navigate the trails of everyday life. You will have a huge edge over most and also a wonderful tool for your continued Synthesis. All it takes is a little daily tuning in; I promise, it's waiting for you.

※ ※ ※

EPILOGUE

It is 7 o'clock on a Friday evening. It's been a long, busy week, and I am beat. I can't wait to get home to a glass of wine and a nice dinner. Just as I'm closing the outer door to the office, the phone rings. I deliberate for a second: Do I answer it or let voice mail take a message so I can deal with the call tomorrow?

"Okay, okay, I'm coming," I mutter. I walk to back my desk and pick up. "Good evening, this is Dr. McGrail," I answer.

"Dr. John, it's me, Michaela. I just landed in Las Vegas, and I'm fine!"

"Excellent, Michaela, that's terrific!"

"It was just amazing. Truthfully, I did get a little nervous right at takeoff, but then I just tuned in and in a second I knew, I simply knew I was going to be okay. I calmed right down and the rest of the flight was a breeze. It really worked!"

"Excellent, Michaela, I'm proud of you! You have a great time and safe trip home, and thanks for calling."

I hang up the phone and leave the office again, except this time I'm leaving with something I hadn't had a minute earlier: a broad smile on my face. I so love it when someone "gets it," and actually experiences the results of the process. It is at this moment people begin to realize just how powerful they are and, even better, how powerful they can be, thus opening up a vast window of opportunity for even greater change, growth, and perhaps transcendence. I call it their second awakening—the first being the realization that changing their life is not only something they want, but also something that's possible. They are learning the dance of Synthesis.

CHAPTER 8 SUMMARY
Takeaways

⇥ The alchemy of change, the transformation, takes place when the conscious energies of the Formula for Change are introduced and integrated into the subconscious, where the programmed knowns reside. Hypnosis and meditation, virtually identical states of consciousness, are perhaps the very best tools that exist to accomplish this.

⇥ Hypnosis is generally thought of as a solution for specific issues and symptoms, whereas meditation is thought of as more for systemic and long-term wellbeing. As such, and because they are natural, safe, painless, and virtually identical states of mind, they fit into the model of Synthesis incredibly well.

⇥ With access to the lower subconscious, we can destroy the barrier to our superconscious energies and strengthen them—particularly spiritual energy, which feeds love and self-esteem, and serves as our connection to inner vision, our powerful, protective, and predictive sixth sense.

⇥ When we learn to tune in to and trust our inner vision, we gain enormous power and control over our choices and outcomes. Inner vision cannot give bad guidance, but its signal must be pure and strong. Only by quieting the mind and shutting out the "outside noise" through regular meditation can we accomplish this strengthening and refinement.

Action Items

⇥ It's time for you to take stock and evaluate your situation, your place in the process. If you've understood everything and have been completing all the assigned action items thus far, just keep doing what you're doing. If there was anything you didn't understand, or if you haven't accomplished and/or begun all the assigned action items, please go back and review the material; re-read the appropriate chapter or sections as necessary, and catch up on the action items.

It is now time to get out of linear mode and into three-dimensional or holistic mode wherein everything happens at the same time. It's also time for you to create your special place. It's really simple to do: Do your 21 breaths, then simply imagine moving toward a place; you might imagine walking down a flight of stairs, or entering through a gate or portal, or floating down from the sky, diving into a pool, swimming through a passage, and coming up on the other side, or entering it in any way that feels good to you. The place itself can be indoors or outside, a real place on Earth or one you simply imagine, or even a combination of the real and imaginary. For instance, mine is a combination of two beaches that I love, one on Cape Cod and one in Kauai, and a special spot in the mountains in Southern California where we love to camp. There is no right way to do it. Just make it your own. Change the features anytime you wish, and remember, when you enter this place in your imagination you can do or be anything. It is the most beautiful, peaceful, and safe place in the world, and in it you are omnipotent! This place in your mind is your personal workshop, laboratory, and spiritual sanctuary. It is here where much of the magic and alchemy of your Synthesis—the creation, blending, balancing, and integration of energies for change, growth, and transformation—occurs.

Chapter 9:
The Dance

I would not know what the spirit of a philosopher might wish more to be than a good dancer.

—Friedrich Nietzsche

It is a humid Tuesday evening in September 1963, and as I stand on the dance floor at the Williams Ballroom Studio, holding a girl in my arms for the first time in my young life, I can feel my heart pounding in my chest. My dance partner is Helen Green, a girl in my 6th-grade class—the girl I have had a crush on since 4th grade and the girl whose suggestion that I attend dancing school came with an implied hint that it might be just the ticket to winning her heart.

Similar to the other 10 or so couples around the room, Helen and I stand in the classic ballroom "closed position." I have my right arm around her waist, lightly resting my hand on the small of her back; her left arm rests on my right shoulder; I hold her right hand in my left; I don't dare make eye contact lest I faint.

This is a moment of magnitude. After seemingly endless practice, counting steps and cadence with our hands held aloft as if around "air partners," we are now paired into real couples and about to attempt our first waltz to music. Mr. Williams stands by the big record player, and at the signal from his wife, a little nod of her head, he gently places the tone-arm on the slowly spinning LP record.

The music begins, my heart rate feels like it doubles—if that's possible—and I feel as though I can hear its pounding over the music. Mrs. Williams, her perfectly coiffed brassy blonde tresses framing a perpetual incandescent smile, stands in the center of the floor. Her voluminous, feminine baritone—a voice that can penetrate any music at any volume—bellows:

"Remember, gentlemen, begin with your left foot forward; ladies, right foot back; ready, and, one-two-three, one-two-three; one-two-three, one-two three," she chants, and simultaneously claps the cadence of the waltz in perfect 3/4 time.

As she intones and claps, we all begin to move like a bunch of wind-up toys, little automatons—stiffly, unsurely, clumsily around in our little box steps; forward side step, back side step, forward side step, back side step, over and over, never moving from our designated spots on the floor. The sheer and total concentration of remembering the sequence of the box step somehow calms me. I begin to actually hear the rhythm of the music. This is almost *fun*. I'm getting the hang of things here, and after two minutes or so it begins to dawn on me: I am actually *dancing*, and even better, *I'm doing it with the girl of my dreams!*

And then, in the blink of an eye, disaster! As Mrs. Williams counts "one," I, a little too eager and maybe just a tad cocky, step forward too quickly and very squarely onto Helen's right foot, which hasn't moved back far or quickly enough to avoid the incursion. With a little squeal of surprise and an audible plop, Helen goes down, landing squarely on her tush. She doesn't let go of me and it's all I can do to miss her as I fall forward and sprawl to the floor.

Instant bedlam! Our cohorts, given an opportunity to release all their pent-up nervous energy do so in the form of a unified roar of prepubescent laughter and a sea of pointing fingers. The music stops. *Oh Lord, please take me now.*

Suffice to say, ours was a very short romance. Helen never forgave me for the indignity, ran off to dance with Kevin Morris, a 7th-grader, and soon thereafter quit dancing school altogether. But for some reason, I stayed with it. I was assigned a new partner, Denise Barclay, whom Mrs. Williams thought made a wonderful match for me.

Denise was a pleasant girl; there were no fireworks between us, but we made a nice couple and danced well together. We practiced twice a week, every week; we added steps, we added technique, we added nuance. Soon we were free of our confining little box steps and gliding about the dance floor with what might actually be called grace and fluidity.

Six months later, in March of 1964 I think it was, Denise and I found ourselves on the dance floor in the grand ballroom of New York's Waldorf Astoria, dancing in our first Dance Masters of America junior competition. We danced the lindy, the fox-trot, the rumba, the tango, the cha-cha, the bossa nova, and finally, the waltz. Ironically, we took first place in the waltz.

As I stood next to Denise, whom I liked okay but certainly didn't love—oh, Helen, what might have been—holding our trophies for the obligatory parental pride photographs, I couldn't help but think of how far I had come in those six months. We continued dancing as a couple, Denise and I, for another three years, right up to ninth grade, improving, progressing, and even winning more competitions. We parted friends, she on her way to cheerleading and drama club, me to football and skiing. And although we didn't know it at the time, those years together had provided a subtle but powerful gift: we had learned the way of the dance.

※   ※   ※

THE DANCE OF SYNTHESIS

Learning to create your new life with Synthesis is a lot like learning to dance. It's a process. You start with the basics, like the box step in the waltz, and then, through consistent and diligent practice, adding steps, technique, and nuance, you improve. You become more skilled, you become more efficient, and you become increasingly more empowered as Synthesis becomes more instinctive.

We are still at the box-step stage; you have been given foundations, the history and theory behind Synthesis, and have been shown the basic steps.

With the takeaway exercises you have been getting used to these steps, sort of like practicing with an air partner. So let's review them quickly and then see about putting it all together—setting the dance of Synthesis to music, so to speak—then adding the nuance and refinement that creates and perpetuates the grace and fluidity of change, empowerment, and, later, transcendence.

First, the conscious energies: You understand now that you create your own reality; everything you think, do, say, and feel is a result of consciousness—your mind—interacting with the environment and responding via the programming or knowns resident in the upper subconscious—the autopilot or engine of behavior.

You have accepted that you are an energy system, and perhaps are growing increasingly comfortable with the concept of thinking of the human organism in terms of three energy streams flowing through the seven energy loci or chakras. This model aids you in recognition, awareness, alignment, orientation, and focusing your efforts for change, growth, health, and wellness.

Most importantly, perhaps, you have recognized that you want to change something or even many things about the way you live your life. You have also taken the time to go within and ensure that what you want to accomplish is truly *for you* and your growth and not because someone else wants it for you; this is the first and most important ingredient in the Formula for Change, and a way of beginning to separate your true self from the influence of mass consciousness and the effects of the seven deadly memes.

You have completed an assessment and prioritization of both your issues and your core values. Hopefully, you have identified the underlying emotional source or causes of your disconnection, and been honest enough to seek assistance in that regard if it's warranted. You have also ensured that your desired changes are in alignment with your core values, really a secondary way of checking that your change is indeed for you and not for someone who claims to know how you should be living your life—yet more tweezing out the real you, whoever that may be. As journalist and poet Christopher Morley said, "There is only one success—to be able to spend your life in your own way." This step helps you find *your* way.

You have consciously decided to completely commit to yourself and the work, the second ingredient in the Formula for Change. You're also purposefully treating yourself with love, honor, and self-respect, questioning the validity of any limiting beliefs or self-deprecating thoughts, and, through the "show me proof" techniques presented in Chapter 7, exposing them for what they most surely are—"Earth-flat" and completely untrue. As a result you have remembered or rediscovered that you are indeed worthy and deserving of anything you wish to have in life. And you are "at cause." You are taking full responsibility for creating whatever it is you desire.

You are sharpening the focus of your energies by adding intention and you are actually expecting that something is going to happen. By this time, if you have been doing all the exercises, you may already be feeling a shift in your energy, your attitudes, and/or feelings about yourself and your issue. It really doesn't take all that much to start the proverbial snowball rolling down the hill.

Now for the unconscious energies: You have been doing the breathing exercise at least once, preferably twice a day and have begun to visualize yourself at the end of the process, having completed the changes you wish to make. You are also taking time to verbalize the affirmations around the process and your worthiness to succeed. In effect, you are communicating to your unconscious mind in its own language—image and imagination—and bridging the conscious and unconscious through affirming in the present tense. Remember, the subconscious only knows present time; you must speak to it thusly.

Whether you have realized it yet or not, that simple breathing exercise—the 21 breaths—is in reality an entrée to the daily quiet time I spoke of in the last chapter. Yes, it is in fact a form of meditation and an introduction to self-hypnosis. In effect, you have already been performing what so many people seem to think is so difficult and mysterious: communicating with and manipulating your subconscious with the most powerful tools known to exist. You have also begun paving the way to a powerful connection with inner vision.

Simply by sitting quietly and taking the time to execute 21 slow, deep, gentle breaths, you purposely trigger what is known as the relaxation response. Your brain orders the secretion of serotonin and dopamine into your system. These are our internal "feel good" drugs. As you relax, your mind grows yet more quiet, and as it does the bombardment and noise from the outside world—the memes of mass consciousness—begin to decrease in both volume and importance; you then travel to your special place.

You begin to connect to your spiritual self, the greater part of you, through inner vision. A reminder: It need not be a vision or an image; it can be perceived as a voice, or a feeling, or a combination similar to a movie. Also remember, its guidance emanates directly from your spirit and your connection to Source and is therefore infallible once purified through consistent practice.

Wow, you have come quite a long way already. You are ready, perhaps eager to put it all to music, yet you may still be feeling a bit awkward, unsteady, and somewhat unsure. *How do I do this dance, really? Is it hard? How do I get good at it? I do not wish to be stuck in the box step, in a linear process; I want to move in three dimensions.*

Indeed, it's time to drop the tone arm and add the music, then add some steps, technique, and nuance so you can begin to Synthesize with grace and fluidity, and prepare yourself to advance, to perform the dance at ever higher levels, thus easily overcoming all seven of the deadly memes and finding your true power.

The easiest way to help you do this, I think, is through an illustrative case study demonstrating the process, resolving a real issue involving a real person, from the outset to the conclusion and beyond. Along the way, we'll discuss all the possible stumbling blocks, setbacks, and bumps in the road that this client had to deal with and overcome in order to succeed—the same ones, by the way, that appear for most clients, in most cases and across most issues. I have chosen this case carefully. It involved an issue most people would think relatively trivial and simple, a very common habit that almost everyone is familiar with in one way or another: nail biting.

NED, NELLY, AND NUBBY NAILS

Ned was a 29-year-old veterinary student who was referred to me by his physician for help in overcoming a chronic and severe nail-biting habit. At his first session Ned reported that he had been biting his nails for as long as he could remember, especially whenever he faced anticipatory anxiety about situations involving meeting strangers and being judged, and/or circumstances in which he was expected to perform, such as making a presentation, attending a business meeting, or doing an interview.

Ned acknowledged that he was feeling nervous and stressed almost constantly as he was preparing for his last two and most difficult final exams and also beginning to schedule employment interviews. He did not want potential employers to see his nails that were bitten to the quick, or "the nubs," as he phrased it; there was actually evidence of bleeding around his cuticles as well.

He was, to use his words, sick of feeling helpless and out of control. His nail biting was so automatic he wouldn't even realize he was doing it until he began to feel pain in his fingertips.

I asked him to think back and really try to pinpoint when this behavior had actually started. His nail biting was clearly only a symptom of a more general insecurity. All he could remember was that as a teenager he had had been diagnosed with attention deficit disorder, commonly known as ADD, shortly after matriculating at a small private high school where he constantly felt inferior to his fellow students.

It seemed that in group study sessions, which were required, he always seemed to be the last and slowest of the group to finish assignments or grasp any material. He was tested and emerged with his "ADD" label and an unremitting feeling of low self-esteem and mild anxiety in any performance situation. This feeling was exacerbated by relentless teasing he received from his peers. They had dubbed him with the derogatory nicknames "Snail" and "Escargot," or "Scarg" for short. Ned related that they had been incessant in their teasing of him.

As Ned reflected, he realized that later, as an undergraduate student, he had done better. He was able to study at his own pace, and his nail biting was much less severe, actually only sporadic, flaring up only during periods of high stress. He also disclosed that his insecurities had returned with a vengeance during vet school, which had once again required that he regularly participate in group or team projects, do more presentations, and now meet with strangers who would be looking at him with a judging eye as he tried to sell himself in his job search.

I decided to handle Ned's situation on two fronts. We would treat the condition symptomatically by creating a subconscious-to-conscious barrier or "trigger" to stop the act of nail biting, and more importantly, we would treat the condition systemically by eradicating his insecurities and helping him reconnect with his self-esteem.

First, the box step. We began with my standard presentation of the models: the Human Hologram (Chapter 2), Quantum Reality Equation (Chapter 3), M4 (Chapter 4), the Human Energy System (Chapter 5), and the Formula for Change (Chapter 7), then introduced him to the focus and relaxation of hypnosis.

Ned responded powerfully to hypnosis, as I find most anxious people do. It has been my experience that people who are prone to chronic anxiety tend to be extremely sensitive, and that usually also equates to excellence in attaining deep trance. Ned proved to fit this pattern and attained a very deep level of relaxation and trance; remember trance is nothing more than focused concentration without conscious distraction, shutting off the naysayer, the critical filter.

After guiding Ned through the crafting of his special place, creating the subconscious-to-conscious barrier or trigger for stopping the act of biting his nails was the first item on our agenda. I suggested to Ned that whenever either hand subconsciously approached his mouth for the purpose of biting his nails, he would become consciously aware of the movement when his fingers reached a distance of about two inches from his teeth. At that point he would "hear" an inner command, "Stop! Drop!" and find his hand dropping away. Ned would then take two or three slow, deep, gentle breaths and find himself feeling very calm and smiling proudly, delighted that he'd caught himself and taken control.

After several repetitions of the trigger sequence while in deep trance, I then began the systemic treatment by having him visualize himself after having made all his changes. Sound familiar? He was to imagine himself feeling calm and in control in those situations that currently triggered stress. He was instructed to imagine himself studying with his group, presenting, and meeting potential employers, and see himself feeling completely at ease. He was instructed to see his fingernails clean and beautifully manicured, an easy smile on his face at all times.

After our trance work, I assigned a homework assignment of a twice-daily exercise of 21 slow, deep, gentle breaths, followed by two visualizations to reinforce what we had just finished. First, he would mentally and physically rehearse the trigger—hand comes up toward mouth, "Stop! Drop!" now breathe deeply and smile. "I'm in control now." Next, he was to visualize himself after we had finished our work together, "There I am, having made all the changes I wanted to make. I am calm, comfortable, and completely at ease in all situations. I am in control, and I like it." Ned was instructed to stay with the visualization until he could "feel" the contentment and happiness of overcoming his issue. We scheduled a session for the following week.

By approaching Ned's condition on two fronts, and assigning a two-part homework assignment, notice we naturally took advantage of the inherent healing attributes of both hypnosis and meditation. After relaxing his mind and body through the 21-breaths exercise, he basically performed hypnosis on himself, neutralizing the specific symptoms of nail biting through the act of practicing the trigger sequence and reminding himself that he was "in control now." He then performed a dynamic meditation through visualizing himself as a finished product—"I am calm, comfortable, and completely at ease in all situations"—thus reinforcing the notion of a systemic energy change and rebalancing.

Advanced Steps

When Ned arrived for his second session, he was in pretty high spirits; he reported having an overall positive week. He reported having bitten his nails on a few occasions, but only for a moment. The rest of the time, the trigger had been successful in thwarting the behavior. He had also solidified a realization that much of his stress was due to constantly worrying what other people thought of him. During the cognitive portion of our session we reviewed the Formula for Change with particular emphasis on the ingredient of self-love, honor, and respect.

We discussed the fact that many studies have been conducted that cast serious doubt on the very existence of ADD and its cousin, attention deficit hyperactivity disorder (ADHD), and I wondered aloud whether Ned had perhaps simply been the victim of owning and identifying himself with nothing more than someone else's label. As I gradually led him into a light trance I suggested that everyone has his or her own personal way of learning and that no one way or speed is particularly better than any other.

I then suggested that he allow himself to drop even deeper into that wonderfully relaxed state, where he would begin to delight in the thought of working at his own pace without worrying how quickly he accomplished his tasks in comparison to others. Doing so would increase both his efficiency and retention.

"In fact," I suggested, "perhaps you will also find it wonderfully freeing to stop comparing yourself to others altogether, or giving any energy to worrying about what they think of you, as you cannot control their thoughts or actions or anything about them. In fact, you may find it compelling to put all your energy into wonderfully and powerfully controlling the only human being you can or will ever be able to control: yourself. And in so doing find how delightful it is to reconnect to and nurture that perfect and abundant unconditional love and self-esteem that eagerly await reawakening in your superconscious."

※ ※ ※

Please re-read that suggestion; this is one of your first and most important advanced steps in mastering the dance of Synthesis: realizing that you can have control over only one person, ever—yourself. You cannot control any other human being on the planet, not even your kids. Oh, sure, you can punish them, ground them, and so on, but you cannot control their minds. Neither can you control your mother or father, brothers or sisters, boyfriend, girlfriend, husband, wife, or friends—only yourself, ever.

So, what other people think, say, or do is what they think, say, or do. How you react to it is *always* your choice, and is a choice you can control. Commit to choosing self-loving, honoring, and respectful choices. If someone doesn't like you, who cares? If someone says something mean or disrespectful, let it go. There are seven billion people on this planet, so there *must* be plenty of people out there who will find you absolutely to their liking, and vice versa.

If you slip and begin to self-disparage at the words or deeds of another—and you may at first—remember the "show me proof" technique: *Is this thought or sentiment expressed about me by another, or that I am thinking as a result of something someone said or did, Earth-round or Earth-flat? Is it true? Must it be true? Does this thought, this choice serve my growth, wellbeing, and the greater good?* If it does, embrace it with all your energy. If not, you owe it to yourself to stop right there and ask, *Why would I do this to myself? This is not following my commitment to love, honor, and respect me.* Then figure out what the empowering choice would be and go for it.

The better you get at living this way, the more empowered you become. The most empowered people anywhere are those who learn to not care at all what anyone thinks of them. They do not do anything in order to garner good will or liking or respect. They concentrate only on being their best selves, making ecological choices, and acting on behalf of their personal growth and the greater good—self-fully.

These empowered ones may use those who are closest to them as sounding boards or reflectors, perhaps, but they never purposely act or behave in any given way or in antithesis of their core values to gain acceptance or favor. For example, I very much care what my wife thinks of me because if I get negative feedback from her I'm almost surely not being my best self; she is a great sounding board/reflector of my projected and internal energy. But at the same time, I never have and never will behave in any given way in order to persuade or encourage her to think well of me. I just concentrate on being my best me. The rest takes care of itself. It will for you too, I promise.

The result of behaving this way, of creating complete self-fullness, is that in doing so you develop and comport yourself with what I like to call a humble confidence, and you become very popular; more people like you and like to be with you, so you get what you and I and all of us want most to begin with: validation and respect. Again, it must always begin from loving and validating yourself from within; it never simply appears or comes from outside sources first. Remember the law of attraction: The universe sends you back whatever energy you project. This represents ultimate control.

In learning to completely love, honor, and respect yourself you will soon discover that any neediness you had in your persona disappears. You rediscover and begin to strengthen your true *self*-esteem. As that occurs you can attract relationships, platonic or otherwise should you so desire, that are based upon sharing energy and mutual empowerment rather than need or filling voids. Needy relationships almost always end up toxic and painful. It is simply impossible to fill a perceived void within you with someone else's energy or power. You cannot control them, so what happens if they change, or withdraw, or simply leave your life? Ouch!

Growing ever stronger and more empowered, and attracting people who like you and are like you—once again simply a function of the law of attraction, birds of a feather flocking together—you naturally find your tribe, your community. Your tribe need not be large; sometimes it begins with only one other person, but it can and will grow as large as you wish, and down goes yet another of the seven deadly memes—isolation.

※ ※ ※

BACK TO NED

At the end of our second session, I added the "show me proof" techniques to Ned's daily homework. We also discussed a dynamic meditation exercise to prepare him for two employment interviews he had scheduled for the following week. One of the great advantages of dynamic meditation is that we can pre-design the way we want events to work out, at least from our perspective. In other words, we can pre-plan how we will behave and how our energy will be projected, controlling that one factor that we can control—ourselves—and thus creating a self-fulfilling prophecy.

Ned was instructed to create two "mind movies" of the interviews, first watching himself from the outside breezing through the interviews in an enthusiastic yet perfectly calm and professional manner, and then experiencing the movie again from his own point of view so he could feel it from within. He was instructed to concentrate on the feeling of being his best self and not caring a bit about what the results would be or the fact that he was being judged. We scheduled a session for two weeks hence. Ned left my office even more enthused than he had been upon arrival.

Two weeks later, Ned arrived for his next session. When I asked how he'd been doing, he reported that he had good news and bad news.

"Give me the good news first," I said.

"Okay," he said, and he extended his hands for my inspection. "Take a look."

Sure enough, there was no evidence of any nail biting. His nails were trimmed and well-manicured, and the surrounding skin had completely healed.

"Excellent," I said. "What else?"

"I had my interviews and they both went really well. I felt really relaxed and sharp. First time I've felt comfortable in that sort of situation in as long as I can remember—maybe ever. Both clinics invited me back for another round, and they went well, too. I believe I'm going to get two offers."

"Even better than I would have hoped!" I exclaimed. "Way to go!"

"Yeah, but..." he said.

"But what? That's awesome," I countered.

"Yeah, but what if they both *do* offer me a job? How do I know which one to take? They're both good companies and I thought I'd be lucky to get even one offer. And just about everyone I know has an opinion and it goes right down the middle. Who do I listen to?"

What a perfect time to add more nuance and technique to Ned's dance. Time to re-explain inner vision, and how it will always guide you in such situations. Ned's instructions were thus: "Simply guide yourself into a quiet, meditative state—the 21 breaths is a great way to do so—and without the distractions from outside influences, you can go within and evaluate which option feels better *to you*. It doesn't matter what anyone else thinks. And remember, inner vision is the guidance of your all-knowing spiritual energy stream. It cannot give you bad advice. It may take a few repetitions at first, but you will get it. Just ask and be open to the signals in whatever form they arrive."

"Okay, doc, I'll take your word for it, and give it a try."

"Excellent. Is that all?" I asked.

"No, there is another issue that's popped up."

WHOA, NELLY!

Ned continued, "It's my girlfriend, Nelly. I've been telling her how great I'm feeling and how much more calm and empowered this is making me and I've been trying to get her to do self-hypnosis and meditation to help her get more motivated to exercise and eat better. She says she wants to lose about 15 pounds, but all she does is talk about it, and then complains that she isn't losing the weight. When I mentioned what I'm doing and showed her my nails, she just shrugged her shoulders and said, 'Good for you, but that stuff is not my gig.' We actually had an argument over it. I mean, I know if she just tries it she'll see the light and it'll be easy for her. I don't get it."

Another perfect technique and nuance moment had dawned. "Ned," I said, "It's time we had a talk about the art and gift of allowance."

"What do you mean?" he asked.

"This is one of the most important lessons I can pass onto you. You must, *must* remember that you cannot control or change anyone, *anyone* else, except yourself. You are the only person you can ever control or change—ever. And when you learn to simply allow others to find their own way *in* their own way, you will have given both them and you one of the greatest gifts you can ever give. They don't feel pressured or put upon, and you don't feel responsible for their lives, because you can't be. Now, if Nelly asks you about it, fine, she's open to hearing it and you can share and show her what you've learned, or have her call someone like me for help. But if she doesn't ask and you try to force it, it cannot have any other outcome than to create discord. As one of my favorite spiritual teachers, Abraham as voiced through Esther Hicks, says, 'You cannot give someone the answers if they are not asking the questions.' You must accept and embrace that fact and allow her to find her way—or not."

"That's it? Just allow her to stay stuck?"

"Well, you have already experienced what happens when you try to convince or change her."

"Yeah, but I can't stand that attitude. I don't want to accept it."

"Allowing is not accepting. There is no resistance in allowing. You don't have to try to accept something that is antithetical to your values; you don't even have to tolerate it because either stance would be painful to you. When you allow, you simply allow. It has no effect upon you whatsoever, and that is peaceful."

"But then she's still overweight and complaining about it."

"Well then, you have to decide whether you're willing to live with that. If so, great; if you cannot, being together may not be a good match for either of you. You have to make choices that serve your growth, and she hers. Her growth is not your job; it's hers. Your growth is not her job; it's yours. You can help one another grow only to the extent that you're both willing to ask the questions that the other can provide answers to and then share the power and do the dance of Synthesis together."

He thought about it for a minute or so and then simply nodded his head. "Okay, I'll think about this. It makes sense to me, but I sure wish she'd ask the questions."

I replied, "Just keep doing what you're doing for yourself. Keep empowering yourself and it will work out exactly the way it's supposed to. As she sees you grow, she may become more curious—or not. We can never tell."

With that, we finished the session with some hypnosis/meditation targeted to helping Ned get comfortable with connecting to inner vision, and focusing on allowing him to allow others to be who and what they are. We scheduled his next session for the following week and called it a day.

* * *

It can be a little difficult to accept the truth of the idea that we really cannot change or control anyone but ourselves, but that is indeed the reality of it. I always remind my clients that our core values—the non-trade-off items in life—are never able to be compromised, at least not peacefully or for very long.

NEXT STOP: PRACTICAL ENLIGHTENMENT

When Ned entered my office for his next session, I couldn't help but notice the changes in him. He walked with a purposeful grace; there was a healthy glow about him. I could see that he was connecting to that state of humble confidence I described earlier, the inevitable result of successfully integrating Synthesis into your life.

Ned gave me a quick update. He had been offered both jobs and had, after several meditations, chosen the smaller of the two clinics, as it afforded a faster track to promotion and both research and eventual management opportunities. This, he had decided, was more important to him and his core values than the higher salary he'd been offered by the other, larger clinic where he would be a staff veterinarian with little advancement opportunity.

He related that many of his friends had urged him to go for the higher-paying position, but he knew—his inner vision knew—that acquiring more responsibility sooner was a better fit for him. He had also decided that Nelly's attitude about her physical condition was something he could live with; they had a very good relationship in other regards, so he had just dropped it and reported that he was working hard on allowing her to find her own way. "It's still not natural to me," he said.

I assured him that with time all of this would be as natural as breathing and that, like any skill, living an empowered, allowing life takes some practice.

"So what's next?" he asked. "When do you finish? When will I be done?"

"Well, I think we'll wrap up today's session with a meditation to balance all three of your energy streams through all seven chakras, and you and I will be done, at least for now; but to answer your question, the truth is you never get it done, at least not until you leave your body in this lifetime."

"Never?" he asked.

"Nope. This is a process that never ends. As you become more empowered, of course, as you accomplish goals, you will create new ones, and continue to grow."

"So what am I supposed to do next?"

"Oh, you'll find it; it will find you, whatever it is. Just allow the process of growing to be the goal, because it's really all we get. We can't relive the past and we can't pre-live the future—though we can always pre-design our days and our major events, and focus our energy upon what we want to achieve. But it's always a process, so celebrate being in it. Use your tools, and enjoy the journey as it unfolds. Keep practicing your dance of Synthesis every day; consistency is the key to getting better and better at it and to evolving as the spiritual being that you and we all are."

"Where does this all lead?" he asked. "How far can I take it?"

"Quite a ways, actually," I replied. "You can take it all the way to practical enlightenment." Ned's eyes widened considerably.

"Enlightenment?" he asked incredulously. "Are you kidding?"

"Not at all, Ned, not at all."

CHAPTER 9 SUMMARY
Takeaways

> ⇥ Learning the art and science of living in Synthesis is very much like learning and choreographing a dance. The models and formulas provide an outline of the basic steps, and with consistent use and practice—plus some nuance and techniques such as the "show me proof" questions to erase self-doubt, tapping into inner vision for guidance, and learning to provide ourselves and others the gift of practicing the art of allowance—we become more proficient and adept; we become more empowered; we become ever more capable of living the life we

desire rather than the one we were programmed for or thought we had to accept. It allows us to overcome the seven deadly memes of mass consciousness and all the disconnection that comes with them. It paves the way for finding our tribe, our community of like-minded souls with whom to share this new lifestyle, and it provides the path to attaining practical enlightenment.

- You can control only one person on the planet, ever, and that is yourself.

- You can change only one person on the planet, ever, and that is yourself.

- When we learn and master the art of allowance—allowing others to be who they are—and take full responsibility for ourselves and how we choose to react to experiences and to what others say and do, it is amazing how much easier our lives become.

Action Items

- Practice, practice, practice! Use your models every day. Include all the conscious energies and techniques with consistent (daily) work on the unconscious through your self-hypnosis/meditation exercises, and tapping into inner vision for guidance in your choices—which choice *feels* better to or for *me*? The more you practice, the more natural and automatic it becomes.

Chapter 10:
Transcendence

As far as we can discern, the sole purpose of human existence is to kindle a light in the darkness of mere being.

—Carl Jung

Ned sat in silence for a moment, and then said, "Really? You're serious? I don't get it. I mean, how can conquering a nail-biting habit possibly lead to something even remotely related to the concept of enlightenment?"

"Tell me," I said, "What does enlightenment mean to you?"

"Well," he replied, "when I think of enlightenment, I immediately think of people such as Jesus, or Buddha, or Mohammed, or, who were those other people you mentioned when we were discussing philosophy and unconditional love?"

"Oh sure, I mentioned Krishna, Babaji, and White Buffalo Woman for the Native Americans. The point was that all cultures have what we might call icons or paragons of absolute enlightenment; those few exceptional beings who encompass not only the essence of our purest emotion, unconditional love, but also what we might call superhuman or divine characteristics while in human form. And we agreed that there are very few of those people who ever have or ever will exist."

"Right," he said.

"And then we also talked about the fact that there are people much more like us, normal human beings, who use and live the teachings of our icons of enlightenment, and essentially transcend the limitations of materialism and spiritual disconnection associated with modern culture; individuals such as Mahatma Gandhi, Mother Theresa, Paramahansa Yogananda, Black Elk, or the Dalai Lama. Would you consider them enlightened?"

"Absolutely," he replied.

"Well that brings the concept closer to home, doesn't it?" I asked.

"I guess so," he said. "But I certainly can't envision *me* being one of them."

"I understand. Even when someone such as Jesus assures us that 'anyone can do what I do and live as I live,' or when Fools Crow, one of the most famous and powerful Native American shamans ever, said basically the same thing—'the power is available to anyone,' which means it is doable for all of us—it takes a very special calling and devotion to evolve that far."

"Exactly," he said. "That's what I mean. So how could I reasonably expect—?"

"Whoa, Ned, hold the phone," I interrupted. "Let's just get *all* the obstacles out of the way. Remember what I said: I said *practical* enlightenment. And I believe anyone can fairly easily attain that state of being."

"Okay," he said, "I'm all ears. So, as Ricky Ricardo used to say, 'Splain!"

"Let's start with the word, *practical*. The dictionary defines *practical* as 'relating to, or manifested in practice, action: not theoretical or ideal: actively engaged in some course of action or occupation.' Fair enough?"

"Sounds good," said Ned.

"Good. Now we both know that enlightenment means many things to many people; its definition is the underpinning, and its attainment is the single-most important aspiration of entire philosophical doctrines, religions, and cultures. As such, it's quite often portrayed or perceived as virtually impossible for us mere mortals to attain."

Ned said, "That's kind of what I meant a minute ago."

"Alright then, let's see if we can find a definition of enlightenment to which we can attach the concept of practical. The dictionary definition of *enlightenment* uses words like *explanation, illumination,* and *clarification.* The Buddha defined it simply as 'the end of suffering.' I really love that definition—simple, poignant, easy to understand."

"Yeah, it is that," said Ned.

"So, let's define *practical enlightenment* as an explanation, illumination, or clarification—knowledge—leveraged through a practice and action that then is able to manifest or result in the end of suffering."

Ned sat in silent thought for a few moments. Nodding, he said, "Sounds reasonable enough."

"Good; I believe that we can find the explanation, illumination, and clarification—the knowledge—in the new science, the quantum model of reality. Remember that?"

"Sure," he replied.

"And the active practice of the methodology and techniques of Synthesis provide a way to leverage that understanding, illumination, and clarification in a very realistic way, enabling us to end our suffering and transcend the seven deadly memes. Remember how we talked about the fact that they are the source of our individual and collective disconnection, and that they all arise from our ingrained and obsessive egocentric focus on lack, the negative side of contrast?"

"Yeah, I remember that," he said.

"Well, through Synthesis, we can all learn to overcome that dark energy, and then turn our lives into an abundant, empowered, joyful, and ecological experience. And in so doing, we can fulfill our true and individual purpose; we can 'kindle a light in the darkness of mere being,' as suggested by Carl Jung. And I believe that we can make that light very, very bright; and *that* can lead to the end of our suffering."

"Still sounds like a pretty tall order," he replied.

"It's not, really," I said. "Tell you what, let's use a real-life example. Let's use you!"

"Me?"

"Why not? You asked the question and you're already well into the process."

"I am?"

"Yes, Ned, you are."

"I'm even more all ears," he said, now with a somewhat more expectant rather than doubtful tone.

"Okay, let's start at the beginning. When you first came in, you were suffering from your nail-biting habit, which was a symptom or reflection of what we could fairly call a self-denigrating attitude—a disconnection—arising from your being labeled as having ADD, and your stress and anxiety around being judged by others. In essence you were suffering from chronic low self-esteem. You felt as if you were, in your words, 'less than.' Would you say that pretty much covers it?"

"Sure," he replied.

"Do you remember the very first thing we discussed, before we started doing any work?" I asked.

"We talked about quantum reality, and you showed me the equation, how we create our own reality through our energy exchanges, and then you explained your models, the Human Energy System, the mind model; what did you call that?"

"M4," I replied.

"Right, M4. You showed me how the mind develops and functions, and how we get stuck. Then you took me through the Formula for Change and showed me how we apply those conscious energies at a subconscious level to change the dynamic, to reprogram my subconscious computer or autopilot, so to speak; to change my subconscious thoughts and beliefs to align with my conscious desires, and create a new reality equation."

"Good! And then?" I asked.

"And then we started working in here with the hypnosis and you assigned my homework, which I now know is consciously applying the Formula for Change, focusing my conscious thoughts on what I want in combination with the daily meditations that create, reinforce, and amplify the subconscious changes."

"Wow, Ned, you were really paying attention. That is excellent!" I exclaimed. "That's what Synthesis is all about—leveraging knowledge and wisdom both ancient and modern, both art and science, to blend, balance, and integrate your conscious and unconscious energies, which then empowers you to manifest whatever you want. Let's break it down a little bit more. First, when we accept and embrace the 'new reality' suggested by quantum science, which, if you remember, is a model of reality that our ancestors intuitively understood and accepted and one modern science is now proving—"

"Yeah, that's pretty cool stuff," he said.

"Indeed it is," I replied. "Well, with that first step, we in fact both accept responsibility for how our life unfolds, and also give ourselves a means to create whatever reality we want. We do it through the purposeful development, manipulation, balance, and integration of our energy streams—physical, emotional, and spiritual—all through the aegis of the law of attraction. Remember, that which is like unto itself is drawn. Or more simply, energy attracts similar energy."

"Right, I like that concept too!" he said.

"So, we now *know* we can get rid of the negative programmed patterns—knowns, or habits, beliefs, and emotions—that don't serve us. In your case (and this is how it works for most of us), you started with something relatively small, by overcoming your nail-biting habit—the symptom. How did accomplishing that make you feel?"

"It felt great," he said. "It gave me a sense of control."

"Right," I replied. "But that step was really just scratching the surface. Think of what else you're learning, and what else has happened for you, what you've accomplished in just a few weeks."

"What do you mean?" he asked.

"Well, you've learned and are learning some very important lessons about empowering your life. You're learning not to worry or care about what other people think of you and you're no longer simply accepting their labels, nor making choices based upon what *they* expect of you."

"Yeah, you're right; that kind of snuck up on me."

"You're learning to choose what feels right for *you*. That means you're learning to tap into and trust the guidance of inner vision. Think of the two job offers and how you handled them, and the choice you made: *your* choice."

"That one really felt good," he said.

"Absolutely, and it will only get better. Now, think about how you finally handled Nelly and her resistance to your desires for her to make changes that she wasn't ready to make. You've learned that you cannot control or change anyone but yourself."

"Oh, I learned that one big-time," he said with a chuckle.

"Right, so that lesson introduced you to the art of allowance: allowing others to be who they are and what they are, because there isn't anything you can do about it, and also not allowing who they are to affect who *you* are. Does practicing allowance feel better to you?" I asked.

"Sure it does," said Ned. "But like I said, it still doesn't feel completely natural to me. I still struggle with some of this, especially in terms of Nelly and our differences. And truthfully, I still often think about what others are thinking of me."

"That is totally okay. Let me gently remind you again that all of this is a process, and you never get it done."

"Not like vet school school, huh?"

"No, this process is ongoing for the rest of your life."

"Does it get easier?" he asked.

"Absolutely, and all it takes is consistent practice. Here's an example: Do you remember what it was like to learn how to walk?"

"Of course not."

"Right, but I can assure you that when you first started trying you fell on your little butt a lot. And you just kept at it because you saw these big versions of you (adults) walking around, and you wanted to do it. So you just kept at it and kept at it, and eventually you got it. Now, tell me, do you ever consciously think about walking now, today?"

"No, never."

"Exactly. The act of walking is absolutely automatic for you now; it's ingrained into your subconscious programming. So while you're walking you can focus on and consciously think about other things, such as where you're going, or how the weather is."

"Ah," he began, "so if I keep practicing all of this, it will become automatic?"

"That's pretty much it. And as we master the basics of being mindful of our choices, of the law of attraction, the law of allowance, and the art of Synthesis, we keep growing and evolving. First, we overcome something small such as nail biting, or smoking, or a fear or phobia, and that gives us proof that we can change. Our Western sensibilities kick in. 'Aha,' we say, 'I've seen results, and now I can believe in the process; I think I'll tackle something else.' And so we do."

"You're right, that's what's happening to me!"

"Yup, you have begun to work on more profound changes. You're reconnecting with self-love and self-esteem, and nurturing and strengthening your spiritual energy. As all of this occurs, you increase the balance and integration among your three energy streams and between the conscious and unconscious. You become super-healthy, physically. Taking care of the body—your space-time suit—by eating well and moving it become compelling choices for you. Emotionally, you learn to keep your ego in check. Remember, it's the ego—I, me—that usually gets us into trouble. You also become spiritually healthy, which is what keeps your ego in balance and appropriately subdued."

"So, am I trying to get rid of my ego?" he asked.

"No, no, no," I replied. "Your ego is what makes you an individual, what makes you special and unique. We don't want it gone; we just want its energy to be balanced so it doesn't run amok. It's all and always about energetic balance."

"Okay, then what?" Ned asked.

"As you continue this process, you also become continually more mindful and more and more aware of your choices. Remember, everything you think, do, say, and feel is the result of choice."

"So..."

"So, eventually you become aware of your choices as you make them, as life events occur. Your conscious and subconscious minds merge and integrate, and work together without much need of the critical filter. You're not spending nearly as much time on autopilot, and when you are, your reprogrammed autopilot is mostly taking you where you want to go. Imagine making empowering choices as events in your life unfold, in real time."

"How does that feel?" asked Ned.

"It's like living in a constant state of meditation. As you do all this, you increasingly project a pure, positive energy; that humble but consummate confidence that makes you very attractive to others. You find your tribe, your community. You then realize you've overcome your focus on lack. You become an empowered creator of abundance; you transcend the seven deadly memes. Life is fun!"

As I finished, I noticed that Ned was sort of staring off into space. Finally he said, "What you describe sounds incredible. And this is really possible?"

"Absolutely possible," I replied. "Just be consistent and embrace the process. Always let the process of obtaining a goal be as important as the goal itself, because—let me repeat this—all we ever really have is process anyway. Life is a process, a constant exchange and interchange of energy between you and your environment, and with Synthesis you're creating and managing that energy exchange; you're living with purpose on purpose."

"Yes, I guess I am."

"So, do you think living your life in this way could lead to an end of your suffering?"

"Well, sure it could," he replied. "But, frankly, it seems to me that it would be hard to maintain that state of being all the time, and that it would take forever to get there."

"That, my young friend, is why it's called *practical* enlightenment. We are, of course, human, and therefore imperfect. The emotional energy of runaway ego will sometimes get the better of all of us; we will all sometimes slip up and have those Earth-flat moments of disconnection. But I promise you that you can get so good at this that those moments occur very rarely. And when they do, they are much less problematic and far shorter in duration because you are so much more aware and in control, and you have the tools and know-how to bring yourself back into balance. So, practically speaking, you can live your life with very little to no suffering, almost all of the time. And Ned, it doesn't have to take very long at all to get there. Remember the wet, sticky snowball rolling down the hill? It gets big and fast pretty quickly."

"Alright," he said. "I get it, and I'm in. All in!"

"Excellent choice!" I said.

※ ※ ※

And thus we come to both an end and a beginning. While we near the end of my story of Synthesis and our journey, our session together, you are just beginning your new journey: the journey of living your life on purpose and with purpose. As I explained to Ned, and as I explain to all my clients, for those who truly embrace and practice the concept of Synthesis, life becomes the extremely wonderful adventure it is supposed to be. Life is supposed to be fun, and now it can be very fun indeed! I have never seen anyone truly commit to the process and not find their life transcended and transformed.

In so doing, we reclaim our birthright and take the very best advantage of the incredibly precious gift of living in physical reality on our beautiful but imperiled planet. Those individuals who stay the course and grow into a state of practical enlightenment also give all of us and the Earth another gift, and thus contribute to a much larger consequence. They become what I call luminaries of enlightened living.

I believe that these luminaries can and will, through their powerful example, attract others to this way of life, and so on and so on, until we trigger a viral proliferation of humanity rediscovering and remembering who we are: children of the universe and part of the energy of Source and all creation. We can then return to living in energetic balance with ourselves, with our fellow men and creatures, and with our Mother Earth, and thus save ourselves and our planet.

That notion raises interesting questions: What is the critical mass needed for this to come about? How many of these luminaries, these practically enlightened individuals, will it take to steer humankind back to the path of the ancients and the icons, living as quantum beings in energetic balance and harmony within and as part of the quantum universe?

I do not know, but I believe it can and must be done. With today's technology and instant global communication, our planet is indeed very small; thus, the concept and possibility of a viral spread of a new mass consciousness does not seem at all far-fetched.

I passionately believe it is very, very much worth the effort because the exceptionally good news is that the process of creating this critical mass of enlightened humanity is so wonderfully positive and empowering for every individual who decides to join the effort. I'm sure you will agree that it's a win-win situation, and a concept that begs just one more question: Are *you* in?

CHAPTER 10 SUMMARY

Takeaways

⇥ Practical enlightenment is a state of living in energetic balance and integration among the physical, emotional, and spiritual energy streams in our Human Energy System. It involves the integration of conscious and unconscious energies into a state of nearly constant mindfulness and awareness. In this state an individual mindfully makes empowering and ecological choices in real time as events unfold, thus creating a wonderfully empowered life experience, transcending the seven deadly memes of mass consciousness, and bringing an end to their disconnection and suffering.

⇥ Practical enlightenment is attainable by anyone willing to commit to onself, embrace one's reality as a quantum being, and then actively undertake and practice a process for manipulating one's quantum energy and the law of attraction.

⇥ Synthesis provides an exceptionally efficient tool set and methodology for embarking upon and maintaining this practice; it can and often does begin with the smallest of changes that can then lead to an enormous energetic proliferation, culminating in the virtual end of suffering and an empowered, joyful life—practical enlightenment—the birthright of every single human being.

Action Items

⇥ Synthesize!

Appendix A: Hypnosis and Meditation Too

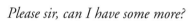

Please sir, can I have some more?
—Oliver Twist

As you now know, nothing occurs in your reality that isn't processed by and through your mind. It's *all* in your mind. And isn't it wonderful that nature has given us the incredibly powerful tools of hypnosis and meditation for balancing and integrating not only our physical, emotional, and spiritual energy streams, but also the dynamic between the conscious and unconscious mind?

Given the perfection of nature there is no surprise here. What *is* sometimes so surprising to me is that so many of us in modern society are so completely unaware of these powerful resources, though it is so easy to take advantage of the potential they offer. Of course, you now know how important hypnosis and meditation can be (perhaps even *must* be) in one's passage to empowerment and beyond. They are the primary tools of Synthesis, and the techniques presented in this book are among the easiest to employ and master.

In fact, you may well find that what I've already given you is all you need. Still, the more I thought about it the more I thought it important to provide you with just a bit more information and some variations on the techniques I've already outlined to help you accelerate your incorporation and use of self-hypnosis and meditation into your life.

I'll begin by reminding you that hypnosis and meditation are extremely similar states of consciousness. The primary difference is really about their traditional associations: Hypnosis is primarily associated with the facilitation of short-term changes in behaviors, beliefs, habits, emotional patterns, and managing assorted physical conditions such as chronic pain. Meditation is traditionally more associated with spiritual development and the long-term, life-long maintenance of energetic balance within oneself, and also between the individual and the outer realm of the universal energy field, what we've called Source Energy or the quantum web.

Given the similarities between these two sates of consciousness—and as you know in my method they are treated as basically one and the same—the techniques an individual uses to enter a hypnotic/meditative state are interchangeable. The common and necessary ingredients are physical relaxation and focused concentration, which lead to a shift in brain activity from the normal frequencies of everyday conscious awareness, called *beta*, into deeper, slower frequencies known as *alpha*, *theta*, and *delta*. In these states our minds become very receptive to learning and change, and allow us to connect to our inner selves without the noise of mass consciousness to distract us.

Very quickly, alpha is associated with a light state of meditation or hypnotic trance, excellent for visualization and projecting your visions and desires into the universal field. Theta is a slower, deeper brainwave frequency, associated with very deep relaxation and awareness; this is the frequency of the sixth sense, of inner vision, wherein you receive insights, visions, answers, and premonitions to help guide your choices in life. Delta is associated with deep sleep; in delta you are in fact sleeping. The dream state occurs in delta, and dreams can be very helpful in guiding our growth and development once we learn how to interpret and analyze them. One word of warning here: those dream dictionaries that claim to provide the meanings of dream symbols are to be used with great caution. We all use and have symbols in our dreams, but my snake and your snake can mean two very different things. It's all about context, of course, and frankly that's really another whole book.

Most of your daily work is accomplished in the alpha and theta states. If you fall into delta, you've fallen asleep, but don't worry when it happens (it almost certainly will). If you attempt to meditate or do some hypnosis and you fall asleep, it just means you were tired and needed a nap. To avoid falling asleep, I recommend you do your daily hypnosis/meditation work while sitting up in a comfortable but erect position. Lying down is just asking to fall asleep for most of us.

WHY MORE TECHNIQUES?

The technique I outline in Chapter 8–21 slow, deep breaths, going to your special place, and then using your mind to picture, visualize, imagine, and feel yourself having accomplished what you wish—is a basic and effective method of dynamic meditation that incorporates all the primary sensory inputs. It works very well for almost everyone. So why present more here?

First, there are many ways of "getting there" (entering a hypnotic/meditative state of mind), and variation keeps things interesting. More important, however, is the fact that although we all use all of our available senses to process our life experiences—visual, auditory, kinesthetic (physical sensations), and olfactory/gustatory (smell and taste)—most of us also have favorites that we rely upon more than the others. Some people are more visually oriented, some are more auditory, and some are more physical or kinesthetic. Thus, the additional techniques and variations I'm about to present are simply to aid you in utilizing your favorite sensory system if you have one, to enhance and accelerate your mastery.

As you progress and get better and quicker at entering your hypnotic/meditative state, you can do your dynamic work and then have more time to spend quietly, going deeper into theta, becoming more mindful and aware, and getting better at tuning into and utilizing inner vision as described in Chapter 8.

The following techniques are grouped—visual, auditory, kinesthetic, olfactory/gustatory, and one that's an amalgam—but feel free to mix and match until you find the methods, techniques, and sequences that work best for you. Remember, you can have fun while you're learning and experimenting.

VISUALS

If you are more visually oriented, it is wonderful to use a visual cue or trigger to help you focus your mind and go within while you're taking your 21 breaths. You might try fixing your gaze upon the flame of a candle, or a spot on the wall in front of you. I would also recommend positioning the object you intend to focus on directly in front of you and above your eye line, meaning that if you sit up with your head level, you must look up with your eyes to find the object. Looking up instantly triggers the beginning of alpha brain activity—just what we want for dynamic meditation and self-hypnosis.

If you're practicing outdoors, in nature—highly recommended—then you might find a running stream and focus upon the flow of the water. Try using a beautiful flower, or a leaf, or a tree. If you can sit next to a very still pool, look into the pool and focus on the stillness of the water, or on one part of the reflected image—maybe even your own.

As you focus and do your breathing, at some point you will notice that whatever you're looking at becomes blurry, or appears as if it's at the end of a dark tunnel, or it may appear to move, almost as if it's breathing. You may also find that your eyes become very heavy as you blink. At some point you find they just want to close, and as you allow them to, you feel that physical shift into your state; time to completely relax and take yourself to your special place to begin your visualization work.

When you have completed your dynamic meditation, your visualization—seeing, being with, and feeling the energy of your new you—you can continue going deeper and tune in to inner vision. Just notice the colors and patterns you see behind your eyelids, and focus on these until you see purple. When you see purple, you are in touch with your spiritual energy; inner vision can now be accessed for guidance, answers, or just a deep and profound period of peace of mind. Just allow, and be aware of thoughts, feelings, images, or even a voice within. With a little practice you will tune in quite well.

AUDITORIES

If you are more auditory in your sensory orientation, and rely more on sound to process your world, then you might find it helpful to use a pleasant repetitive sound pattern to facilitate your shift in consciousness from alert and awake beta to the deeper, quieter alpha and theta states. Examples would be soothing instrumental New Age music, quiet chanting, rhythmic drumming, or sound effects such as wind chimes. I especially like the sounds of nature, such as gently falling rain, birds singing, chirping crickets or frogs, crashing surf, a waterfall, or perhaps—and this is one of my very favorites—the sound of a little stream perhaps flowing through the woods.

Any of these repetitive and soothing sound patterns can help you quiet your mind and relax your body as you count down your 21 breaths. You also might consider doing your own quiet or silent chanting of a single word or pair or words—a mantra—to help you go within. Mantras are usually associated with the technique called transcendental meditation, and are assigned by your instructor, but you can certainly choose your own if you are moved to.

What will usually happen when using sound as your focal point is that as you go deeper, the sound will gradually fade into the background and you will feel continually more present and aware of yourself. When that feeling occurs, you know it's time to go to your place and begin your work for the day.

For auditories, once your dynamic meditation work is completed, or if you wish to go deeper and tune in to inner vision, bring yourself back to the sounds. Focus upon the sound itself until you feel as though it is inside you, that it *is* you, and you are it—there is nothing else but the sound and your most inner, predictive, and protective notions. Sometimes you may find that to your delight the more you try to concentrate on the sounds, the quieter they become until you can no longer hear the background sounds; you are in complete silence. In either case, it is now that inner vision can and will sing to you. As always, allow, allow, allow, without judgment, whatever comes to you, in whatever fashion. Then test it: How does this feel to me? The answer and course of action will be obvious.

KINESTHETICS

If you are a feeler, someone who relies heavily upon physical feelings to process experiences, there are a variety of simple and effective techniques you can employ to aid you on your journey within. One of the first techniques I learned more than 30 years ago and still use today is to sit upright, with your hands either on the arms of your chair or resting gently, palms down, on your thighs.

Begin your deep, slow, gentle breathing and focus not so much on counting your breaths, but instead on the very *feeling* of your breathing. Feel the sensation of the air as it enters and leaves your body; feel it passing through your nostrils breathing in, and over your lips breathing out. Then, after a few gentle breaths, bring all your attention to the feelings and sensations in your forefingers—the ones next to your thumbs—just those two fingers. Feel the texture of the fabric of the chair or your clothing, the temperature, and any internal feelings or sensations in the fingers themselves, such as tingling or twitching.

Then, decide which of your two forefingers feels lighter, and now bring all your attention to just that one finger and everything you're feeling in it. Imagine that with every little sensation, it grows lighter and lighter, and get ready, for to your delight and amusement it may well begin to rise up, in small, jerky motions, all by itself without you doing anything but visualizing and thinking about it.

This unconscious or automatic levitation is called an ideomotor response, and it signals that you're shifting into a deeper, quieter state of consciousness. When your finger can rise no higher, you can let it drop or let the feeling of lightness travel up your arm and let your arm levitate as well, until you feel that very profound sense of quiet and presence within. Then, gently let it down if you wish (it's generally more comfortable to do so) and go to your special place for your visualization work.

Another powerful and easy physical trigger is to close your eyes and focus all your attention on completely relaxing your eyelids. With each and every gentle breath you let them relax more and more, until, to your delight and amusement you find that they simply will not work: as long as you hold onto the relaxation, you cannot open your eyes; the harder you try, the more relaxed they become. Let that same feeling flow throughout the rest of your body. It is now time to go to your place.

Reaching inner vision for the kinesthetic is often a matter of focusing so profoundly on your breathing, or one small part of your body, such as a finger or a toe, your eyes, or even a single hair, that you lose touch with all other sensations; it's as if your tactile senses shut down. You know your body is there, but you simply cannot feel it. Or, you can focus all your attention upon your slow, gentle breathing until you can actually feel and almost hear your heart beating. Inner vision is waiting for you. For you the guidance may be a feeling or a sensation; allow and test the feeling. Will this choice serve my growth, my wellbeing, and the greater good?

OLFACTORY/GUSTATORYS

There are very few of us who rely mostly upon our sense of smell and taste; these senses are most often adjunctive in processing our experiences. The exceptions are found mostly in those individuals who pursue careers in the food and beverage industry. Professionals like chefs, vintners, cheese makers, and so on rely on these senses heavily, perhaps almost exclusively in their given vocations. However, for the purpose of meditation and hypnosis, my experience has been that for these people, including a very pleasant aroma or flavor such as a scented candle or incense can be helpful in quieting the mind while also using the visual, auditory, or kinesthetic techniques.

PROGRESSIVE RELAXATION

Progressive relaxation is a technique that utilizes all of our sensory inputs; it is therefore useful for just about anyone. It is also a very easy technique to master as an adjunct to your 21 breaths for going deeper into meditation or hypnosis. Sit comfortably or lie down quietly if you prefer—and again here, a gentle warning: lying down often leads to falling asleep. Do your 21 slow, deep, gentle breaths, and then, with your eyes closed, simply imagine or visualize a beautiful, warm, soothing, colored energy entering your body. If you are sitting upright, begin at the top of your head and work down. If you're lying down, begin at your feet and work up. I'm going to describe it as if you are sitting upright.

Breathe in, slowly, gently, and deeply, and at the top hold the breath for just a moment. Then, as you slowly release the breath, imagine this soothing energy flowing from your forehead throughout every cell, muscle, bone, tissue, and fiber of your head, temples, eyes, and especially your jaw. Let the muscles relax completely; just let go. Imagine the bones and muscles turning to jelly, completely releasing.

With each breath you bring the energy into the next section of your body. After your head and jaw comes the neck, then your shoulders, arms, and hands, the torso and chest, including all your internal organs, and on down— lower abdomen, hips, upper legs and thighs, calves and shins, and finally, your feet from your heels to your toes. By the time you reach your toes (or your head if you did it lying down and worked from the feet up) you are ready to go to your place and do your work.

FINAL THOUGHTS

It's important to remind you that all of these techniques are effective. There is no right or wrong way to do this work. For instance, just because you are more visually oriented does not mean the other techniques will not be effective or fun. Try them all, and again, feel free to play with it. Mix and match until you find the technique(s) and sequence(s) that work best for you. After more than 30 years I use a variety of techniques to keep the process interesting.

The most important thing besides finding a method that works is to *be consistent* in your practice. As I instructed in the book, you must commit to doing it every day, or very nearly so. You are human and life is life; there may well be some days you miss. Still, think about how you treat your physical body; take eating, for example. You don't eat every other or every third day and stay healthy; you don't eat six times one day and skip three days, or breathe only one or two days a week. For Synthesis to work, you must apply it consistently and faithfully; commit to practicing at least once a day.

Know that some days will be better than others. Thoughts from the conscious mind and your everyday world and mass consciousness will try to distract you. Just acknowledge them and let them pass without judgment or self-scolding. The thoughts will slow down and finally stop. Remember, it's your mind, you own it, and now you're re-learning how to drive it. Be patient and kind to yourself always. As with any skill, the more you practice, the better at it you will get. There is no one, and I do mean no one, who cannot become very skilled and adept at strengthening, nurturing, balancing, and integrating their energy streams. With consistent practice you will soon find that you can enter that delightful state of consciousness almost instantly, and be tuning in to inner vision in real time.

Finally, the techniques I've presented here and in the body of the book, although highly effective for almost everyone, are still only just scratching the surface of many variations and techniques for entering and utilizing a meditative/hypnotic state. If you are interested in learning more, and I very much hope you are, you will find some excellent sources of information in Appendix C. Happy exploring!

Appendix B:
Need a Hand?

You cannot teach a man anything; you can only help him find it within himself.

—Galileo Galilei

Synthesis has been presented in this book as a self-facilitated process. It is a process designed to achieve what Galileo's quote acknowledges: to help you discover or rediscover and then utilize the resources within you—and they *are* within you—to get your life working the way you want it to be working, to take you to personal empowerment and beyond if you choose to go there. It is your birthright to live so.

All that said, as I discussed in Chapter 6, there are some steps in the process that can be difficult for some people to accomplish on their own. For instance, in order to really let go of your limiting beliefs, emotions, and behaviors you must be able to objectively assess yourself, identify the cause or causes, visualize and imagine the new you, and be able to switch your thinking from being "at effect," the so-called victim of circumstance, to being "at cause," taking responsibility for your condition and your cure. And in truth, some people need some help with that vital step.

Some people may also find that teaching themselves hypnosis and meditation through doing the exercises and trying the techniques in a book may not be easy. In either case, if you feel you need assistance then you owe it to yourself to get it. To repeat an earlier point, it's your life, your happiness, and your empowerment. You deserve to have it, and if you need help, it's out there. So, how do you find it?

The process of finding a good therapist or hypnotherapist is really no different than that for finding any service professional. Assuming you are interested in working within the realm of what we've discussed in this book (working at both a conscious and subconscious level, and using the power of hypnosis and meditation to help you instill a lasting change), you will probably do best with a qualified hypnotherapist, and to take it a step further, I would add that you'd do best with someone who is spiritually oriented. Remember, spirituality is an integral part of your essence; this has nothing to do with religion. Spirituality is completely non-denominational. Source has no favorites.

Perhaps the best and easiest way to start your search is to ask friends, relatives, and colleagues for a personal referral. If you know someone who had used these services, you are ahead of the game. If not, or if you do not feel comfortable asking about such things, and that is quite alright, then you have to find your therapist on your own. Here are some guidelines.

First, look to see who is in practice in your area. In this day and age, many if not most practitioners have Websites. Find several in your area through a Web search and take a look at their sites. You can learn a lot by the look and feel of a Website. Check the person's bio, including training and credentials if they are listed—and they should be—and always look for client testimonials. No guarantee here, but if there are none, I'd be very wary. I would recommend you plan on calling four or five people in your area if that's possible.

When you call, ask the person about his or her training and experience. Most states have no rigorous regulations governing the training or qualifications of hypnosis practitioners. This means that anyone can call him- or herself a therapeutic hypnotist or hypnotherapist, and there are a lot of training programs out there that will qualify an individual as such with little actual training or experience. When you ask about this, any good practitioner should be forthcoming. Ask how long they've been in practice; being new doesn't mean they aren't any good. In fact, someone who is newer to the field and well trained has the benefit of having learned all the latest techniques.

A poorly trained or incompetent practitioner can't hurt you; hypnosis and meditation are completely natural states of consciousness. In other words, no one can damage your mind with hypnosis or meditation, but if a practitioner is not well trained and is not very experienced, he or she may not be able to help you very much.

Ask practitioners about specialties and about their experience working with your particular issue. ASK FOR CLIENT REFERENCES! Any practitioner who refuses to offer you a chance to speak to clients whom he or she has worked with (and hopefully on a similar issue) is one I would recommend you avoid. It is absolutely possible to speak to people without jeopardizing their confidentiality, and most clients who got good results from working with someone are only too happy to speak to potential new clients. If your candidate therapist offers references, you probably have a professional and reputable practitioner. You might not even feel as though you need to call the references; that's totally your option, of course.

Finally, ask about fees. This really should be the last question you ask. Fees will vary widely among practitioners and geographies. As a rule, the people who are better at this, who can actually help you get real results more quickly, tend to charge more money because they put a lot of time, effort, and expense into getting good at what they do. The bottom line here is that, similar to most professional services, you tend to get what you pay for.

Most professionals charge by the session or hour; some may offer to sell you blocks of sessions at discounted fees, but because we never really know how many sessions a given client will need, I personally would avoid that in the beginning, even if it sounds as though you will save some money. I personally never offer block discounts to clients until I know them a little and can get a feel for their needs. If, once I begin working with a new client, I feel for some reason that he or she will need more than my average number of sessions, we might discuss his or her purchasing blocks of sessions at discounted fees. Every practitioner does this his or her own way; this way just happens to be mine. As to the required number of sessions, again it is important to remember that every mind is different and responds at its own pace. In general, hypnotherapy is considered a short-term therapy; most people do well pretty quickly. But, if you ask about the number of sessions and it sounds too good to be true...well, it probably is, so be wary of big promises—or *any* promises for that matter.

The only treatment I guarantee in any way is smoking cessation, and even then it's only a guarantee if a client follows my program and does everything I ask of him or her; he or she will receive any extra sessions he or she might need at no charge. Notice I don't guarantee the client *will* quit smoking, only that I will work with him or her beyond the limits of the normal program if he or she wants and need more. Hardly anyone ever does, because the program I use works so well, but in truth not every single client I work with is successful.

Because this work is so very personal, it is vital that you feel that the person you are going to work with is professional, qualified, and competent, and will give you the best care. You have to feel you can be absolutely open and honest; anything less will not do if you want results. After you have spoken to several practitioners, asked all your questions and hopefully gotten satisfactory answers, you hopefully will have a feeling about the one you think is the best fit for you. This is an inner vision moment; trust your gut. And if that practitioner charges a little more than some of the others, remember, it will almost surely take fewer sessions to get where you want to be with a person you feel comfortable with who is a highly experienced and/or highly talented practitioner. Such people usually cost more, but it will be worth it when you are on the other side and synthesizing your new life.

One last note: depending upon your issue, if you are working with something that is either a medical condition or a diagnosed psychogenic condition or disorder—such as clinical depression, anxiety disorder, obsessive-compulsive disorder, IBS, or cancer—and you are going to be working with a lay hypnotherapist (that's one who *is not* licensed to practice medicine or psychotherapy—and they should be forthcoming about that), in most states, such as my home state of California, it is a law that they and you obtain a written referral from a licensed physician or mental health practitioner before beginning the work. This law is meant to protect you, the consumer. If a hypnotherapist or spiritual teacher is not a physician or licensed as a psychotherapist, and he or she is willing to work on a diagnosed condition without an appropriate written referral, I have two words of advice: Don't go!

Most of the time this is simply a formality, but it is important, because hypnosis and meditation can mask physical symptoms. For instance, if someone comes to me with a headache and I help him or her ease the discomfort or make it go away completely (often in a matter of a few minutes), and that headache was caused by a tumor, I haven't done the client any favors—in fact, perhaps quite the opposite. The bottom line is that it is important that we do not mask medical symptoms, or treat mental health conditions we aren't qualified to treat. Don't compromise your health and wellbeing; it usually takes nothing more than a phone call to your doctor, psychiatrist, or psychologist, and a simple signed statement stating that hypnosis *will not be harmful to you.*

Your doctor doesn't have to believe in it; that's your decision, but most healthcare professionals recognize that for just about anyone and everyone, hypnosis and mind/body/spiritual balancing cannot do any harm. There are a very few conditions that would qualify as exceptions (for example, schizophrenia), and we want to make sure we don't miss one of them. Any competent, well-trained hypnosis professional will not even consider working on such a medical or psychogenic condition without this vital step being taken care of. They would not even think of compromising your health and wellbeing, ever, so don't you do it either.

With blessings,

John

Appendix C:
Additional Resources

Properly, we should read for power. Man reading should be man intensely alive. The book should be a ball of light in one's hand.

—Ezra Pound

One of the many reasons I wrote *The Synthesis Effect* was to motivate and spark as many people as possible to learn just how powerful we are and how powerful we can become. And as I have mentioned earlier, I didn't just learn what I know, nor develop my method of Synthesis in a vacuum. I've had the pleasure of reading the works and even meeting and working with some of the great thinkers in the field of quantum reality, spirituality, hypnosis and meditation, personal growth, and human development.

Many of my clients ask me to provide titles of works to help them increase their knowledge and, with that, speed their journey and empowerment even more. If you too are interested in learning more about these subjects, the following resources will get you started. And to reiterate what I stated in the book, this list just scratches the surface. There are a myriad of great works out there. This list is presented by subject matter in roughly the same order as the various subjects appeared in the text. All the following books, films, and other resources are listed in alphabetical order by author, or in the case of a film, by producer. If you see a book listed under multiple categories, it's because it covers more than one subject well. Enjoy!

QUANTUM REALITY

Arntz, William, Betsy Chasse, Matthew Hoffman, and Mark Vicente. *What the Bleep Do We Know?*, DVD. Directed by William Arntz, Betsy Chasse, and Mark Vicente. Los Angeles: 20th Century Fox, 2005.

Braden, Gregg. *The Divine Matrix.* Carlsbad, Calif.: Hay House, 2007.

Lipton, Bruce H. *The Biology of Belief.* Santa Rosa, Calif.: Mountain of Love/Elite Books, 2005.

McTaggart, Lynne. *The Field.* New York: Harper, 2008.

Talbot, Michael. *The Holographic Universe.* New York: HarperCollins, 1991.

THE LAW OF ATTRACTION

Hicks, Jerry, and Esther. *Ask and it Is Given.* Carlsbad, Calif.: Hay House, 2004.

Hicks, Jerry, and Esther. *Manifest Your Desires.* Carlsbad, Calif.: Hay House, 2008.

HUMAN ENERGY: THE CHAKRAS

Myss, Caroline. *Anatomy of the Spirit: The Seven Stages of Power and Healing.* New York: Three Rivers Press, 1996.

Redmond, Layne. *Chakra Meditation.* Boulder, Colo.: Sounds True, 2004.

THE FORMULA FOR CHANGE—INGREDIENTS

Dyer, Wayne. *The Power of Intention.* Carlsbad, Calif.: Hay House, 2004.

Holmes, Ernest. *The Science of Mind.* New York: HarperCollins, 1938.

Katie, Byron, and Stephen Mitchell. *A Thousand Names for Joy: Living in Harmony With the Way Things Are.* New York: Three Rivers Press, 2007.

McTaggart, Lynne. *The Intention Experiment*. New York: Free Press, 2007.

Tolle, Eckhart. *The Power of Now*. Novato, Calif.: New World Library, 1999.

HYPNOSIS AND MEDITATION

Brown, Tom, Jr. *Awakening Spirits*. New York: Berkley, 1994.

Dyer, Wayne. *Getting in the Gap: Making Conscious Contact With God Through Meditation*. Carlsbad, Calif.: Hay House, 2003.

Kabat-Zinn, Jon. *Wherever You Go, There You Are*. New York: Hyperion, 1994.

Kappas, John G. *Professional Hypnotism Manual*. Los Angeles: Panorama Publishing, 1999.

Kroger, William S. *Clinical and Experimental Hypnosis*. Philadelphia: Lippincott, Williams & Wilkins, 1977.

Stockwell, Shelley Lessin. *Hypnosis: How to Put a Smile on Your Face and Money in Your Pocket*. Rancho Palos Verdes: Creativity Unlimited Press, 2000.

SPIRITUALITY, INNER VISION, HEALING

Atwood, Mary Dean. *Spirit Healing: Native American Magic and Medicine*. New York: Sterling, 1991.

Brown, Tom, Jr. *Awakening Spirits*. New York: Berkley, 1994.

Cleary, Thomas. *The Essential Tao*. Edison, N.J.: Castle Books, 1992.

Geller, Uri. *Mind Medicine: The Secret of Powerful Healing*. Boston: Element Books, 1999.

Hay, Louise. *You Can Heal Your Life*. Carlsbad, Calif.: Hay House, 1987.

Hoff, Benjamin. *The Tao of Pooh*. New York: Penguin Books, 1982.

Mails, Thomas E. *Fools Crow: Wisdom and Power*. Tulsa, Okla.: Council Oak Books, 1991.

Notes

CHAPTER 1

1. Retrieved from an online abstract of that symposium that appeared on the Orantia Book Fellowship's Website, *http:// urantiabook.org/archive/science/binion1.htm*.
2. Braden, *The Divine Matrix*.
3. Lipton, *Biology of Belief*, p. 185.
4. Mails, *Fools Crow: Wisdom and Power*, p. 81.
5. Lipton, *Biology of Belief*, p. 185.
6. Kleppner and Jakiw, *One Hundred Years*.
7. Ibid.
8. Ibid.
9. Talbot, *Holographic Universe*, p. 6.
10. Ibid.

CHAPTER 2

1. Talbot, *Holographic Universe*, p. 38.

2. Braden, *Divine Matrix*, p. 56.

3. Misra, "Stone-Age."

4. Brown, *Awakening*, p. 72.

5. For more information, see *www.abraham-hicks.com*.

CHAPTER 5

1. Myss, *The Anatomy of the Spirit*, p. 40.

CHAPTER 8

1. Covey, *Living*, p. 47.

2. Brown, *Awakening*, p. 133.

Bibliography

Braden, Gregg. *The Divine Matrix*. Carlsbad, Calif.: Hay House, 2007.

Brown, Tom, Jr. *Awakening Spirits*. New York: Berkley, 1994.

Covey, Stephen. *Living the 7 Habits: Stories of Courage and Inspiration*. London: Simon & Schuster, 2000.

Kleppner, D., and R. Jakiw. *One Hundred Years of Quantum Physics*. American Association for the Advancement of Science, 2000. Retrieved August 7, 2008, from *www.4physics.com/phy_demo/QM_Article/article.html*.

Lipton, Bruce. *The Biology of Belief*. Santa Rosa, Calif.: Mountain of Love/ Elite Books, 2005. p 185.

Mails, Thomas. Fools Crow: *Wisdom and Power*. Tulsa, Okla.: Council of Oak Books, 1991. p. 81.

Misra, Neelesh. "Stone-Age Cultures Survive Tsunami Waves." Port Plair, India: Associated Press, 2005. Retrieved June 7, 2008, from *www.msnbc .com/id/6786476/*.

Myss, Caroline. *Anatomy of the Spirit: The Seven Stages of Power and Healing*. New York: Three Rivers Press, 1996.

Talbot, Michael. *The Holographic Universe*. New York: HarperCollins, 1991.

Index

About the Author

Dr. John McGrail is clinical hypnotherapist, self-improvement expert, and spiritual teacher. His unique therapeutic and teaching approach blends a life-long passion for understanding the human condition and spirituality with the experience and wisdom acquired through working with thousands of clients and students from all walks of life in his clinical practice and self-improvement/motivational seminars and workshops. His writing and expertise have been featured in *Cosmopolitan*, *Redbook*, *SELF*, *Women First*, *Experience Life*, *Whole Life Times*, WebMD, LIVESTRONG.com, and Videojug.com, and he has been a featured expert on a variety of TV and radio programs.

Dr. McGrail earned a BS degree from Cornell University and did graduate work in communication arts while serving as a commissioned officer and aviator in the United States Coast Guard. After distinguished careers in both military and commercial aviation and mass communications—film, television, and multimedia—he earned his certification in clinical hypnotherapy at the Hypnosis Motivation Institute (HMI), the nation's first federally accredited college of hypnotherapy. He graduated with honors and was cited for outstanding academic and clinical achievement. He is frequently invited back as a guest speaker and student career consultant. After HMI, he went on to earn a PhD in Clinical Hypnotherapy from Breyer State University.

His Websites are *www.drjohnmcgrail.com* and *www.hypnotherapylosangeles. com*. Dr. McGrail and his wife, Lynne-Anne, reside in Los Angeles, California. He is an avid blue-water fisherman, and also enjoys golf, hiking, camping, and the study and exploration of native philosophy and spirituality.